T0320676

China's Formal Online Education under COVID-19

This book investigates how schools, enterprises, and families in China have coped with formal online education in light of government policy throughout the COVID-19 pandemic outbreak, with a special focus on the problems they have encountered and possible solutions.

Using grounded theory, more than 1,000 posts retrieved from public online forums were analyzed under a 4*4 framework, referring to four special time nodes (the proposal period, exploratory period, fully deployed period, and exit period) and four major subjects (government, schools, enterprises, and families). The book identifies four main issues faced by massive implementation of online education during the pandemic: platform selection during the proposal period, teacher training in the exploratory period, resource integration during the fully deployed period, and the flexibility to return to school during the exit period. These findings provide a deeper understanding of the process of online learning in an educational emergency, helping to develop the best countermeasures to be taken in similar situations, as well as providing paths for other countries to follow.

The book will appeal to teachers, researchers, and school administrators of online education and education emergency management, as well as those who are interested in Chinese education during the COVID-19 outbreak in general.

Zehui Zhan is a professor and doctoral supervisor at the School of Information Technology in Education at South China Normal University. She is a Youth Pearl River Scholar, Hong Kong Scholar, and PI of the smart educational equipment industry–university–research cooperation base. She has published more than 50 papers and two textbooks in the field, and received other honors, such as the annual award of excellence in university teaching from the Fok Yingdong Education Foundation and the Ministry of Education in China, the title of best teacher achieving the highest teaching quality, and first prize at the national education software competition. Her major research interests include learning science and STEAM education.

Liming Huo is a postgraduate student at the School of Information Technology in Education, South China Normal University, and also a teacher at the Foshan Meisha Bilingual School, Foshan, Guangdong, whose research interests are STEAM education, programming education, and smart education.

Xiao Yao is a second-year postgraduate student at the School of Information Technology in Education, South China Normal University, whose research interests are STEAM Education, artificial intelligence education, and smart education.

Baichang Zhong is a professor at the School of Information Technology in Education at South China Normal University. He has published more than 160 academic papers in major Chinese and international journals indexed by CSSCI and SSCI, in the field of educational technology. He received the 5th National Excellent Supervisor of M.Ed. in China in 2016. His major research interests include robotics education, STEM education, and online K-12 education.

China Perspectives

The *China Perspectives* series focuses on translating and publishing works by leading Chinese scholars, writing about both global topics and China-related themes. It covers Humanities & Social Sciences, Education, and Media and Psychology, as well as many interdisciplinary themes.

This is the first time any of these books have been published in English for international readers. The series aims to put forward a Chinese perspective, give insights into cutting-edge academic thinking in China, and inspire researchers globally.

To submit proposals, please contact the Taylor & Francis Publisher for China Publishing Programme, Lian Sun (Lian.Sun@informa.com)

Titles in education currently include:

No School Left Behind
Implementation of China's New Mathematics Curriculum Reform (2000–2020)
Wei Gao and Xianwei Liu

China's Formal Online Education under COVID-19
Actions from Government, Schools, Enterprises, and Families
Zehui Zhan, Liming Huo, Xiao Yao and Baichang Zhong

Constructing Social Support System for Left-Behind and Migrant Children in China
Ling Li

The Educational Hopes and Ambitions of "Left-Behind Children" in Rural China
An Ethnographic Case Study
Yang Hong

China Urban and Rural Public Education Service Equalization
Development and Application of Performance Measurement
Luo Zhe

For more information, please visit https://www.routledge.com/China-Perspectives/book-series/CPH

China's Formal Online Education under COVID-19

Actions from Government, Schools,
Enterprises, and Families

**Zehui Zhan, Liming Huo, Xiao Yao and
Baichang Zhong**

LONDON AND NEW YORK

First published 2022
by Routledge
2 Park Square, Milton Park, Abingdon, Oxon OX14 4RN

and by Routledge
605 Third Avenue, New York, NY 10158

Routledge is an imprint of the Taylor & Francis Group, an informa business

British Library Cataloguing in Publication Data
A catalogue record for this book is available from the British Library

Library of Congress Cataloging in Publication Data
A catalog record for this book has been requested

ISBN: 978-1-032-03623-6 (hbk)
ISBN: 978-1-032-03628-1 (pbk)
ISBN: 978-1-003-18826-1 (ebk)

DOI: 10.4324/9781003188261

Typeset in Times New Roman
by SPi Technologies India Pvt Ltd (Straive)

Contents

Figures

Tables

Acknowledgments

Thanks to those who have supported the writing of this book. We would especially like to thank Ma Shuyao, an undergraduate at the College of Computer Information Engineering, Jiangxi Normal University, for her support and contributions to the translation and manuscript proofreading of some chapters, and also Lv Lin, an undergraduate at the School of Information Technology in Education, Anhui Normal University, for her support and contribution to the translation and manuscript proofreading of this book.

We would also like to thank Li Yuanmin and Yuan Xinyue, postgraduates at the School of Information Technology in Education, South China Normal University, for their contributions to the data analysis and coding work.

1 Introduction

The deadly COVID-19 pandemic has had a great impact in education sectors around the world. According to UNESCO, 130 countries have closed schools nationwide, keeping more than 776.7 million children and youth out of schools. As of late April 2020, 1.2 billion (73.8% worldwide) students and youth across the planet have been affected by school and university closures due to the COVID-19 outbreak. Global school closures in response to COVID-19 have exacerbated an already worrisome learning crisis – some 325 million children in many countries across East Asia and the Pacific have now missed more than two months of school. China is the first nation to take action to promote flexible education during the pandemic. Since January 23, 2020, the government of China (GOC) has banned most face-to-face activities, including in-school teaching. In addition, the Chinese Ministry of Education has launched an initiative entitled "Disrupted Classes, Undisrupted Learning" to provide flexible online learning to over 270 million students from their homes. Consequently, government policies have shifted K-12 mainstream education from offline schooling to formal online learning. Many schools have ramped up online classes, to keep students' learning on schedule. Hundreds of millions of adolescents in China have been receiving online education as the only approach to formal learning for four to eight hours a day.

Most governments around the world have temporarily closed educational institutions, in an attempt to contain the spread of the COVID-19 pandemic. These nationwide closures are impacting more than 89% of the world's student population. Several other countries have implemented localized closures impacting millions of additional learners.

To meet the new demand, many solutions have been proposed, such as online flipped classrooms, live broadcasts with interaction, teacher-oriented teaching online with parental assistance offline, multi-platform blended learning, etc. More important, these various forms of online teaching tremendously changed traditional teaching and learning forms. After the proposal period, teachers and students gradually adapted to online learning. It was reasonable to deduce that after the outbreak, when returning to campus, more teachers and students would continue to use the online approach, because the whole process has accumulated rich experience and quality

DOI: 10.4324/9781003188261-1

resources for formal education. In addition, another important and far-reaching influence was the engagement of enterprises related to online education. This closed the gap between schools and enterprise, and shaped a new school-enterprise cooperation form, providing good external conditions to move from informal online learning outside of school to formal online learning inside of school. In brief, COVID-19 has blurred the boundary between formal and informal learning, remodeled the relationships between students, teachers, and schools, and stimulated a significant revolution of educational modality in human history.

We believe that online educational issues under the current outbreak of COVID-19 in China should be specifically addressed. More and more countries and regions will face similar problems, and the experiences from China could be available to them.

To this end, we analyze online education policies and discussions from various parts of society. As we all know, the flexible online learning policy under COVID-19 has aroused a strong response from the public, and policy promotion was actually a dynamic process. Teachers and students are directly involved, and schools, enterprises, and families also respond timely to the policy and interact closely as stakeholders. During the whole period, there have been tremendous public online discussions on online forums, Twitter, blogs, in newspapers, etc., which provide representative samples for discourse analysis.

Therefore, this book tries to figure out: How have schools, enterprises, teachers, and families taken action under government policies in different periods during the COVID-19 pandemic? What kinds of problems have they encountered, and what suggestions have they proposed?

Global disasters have brought huge economic losses and casualties to countries and regions around the world (Ritchie & Roser, 2020; WMO, 2013), and their impact on various countries has shown an upward trend (Cao, 2014; Wu, Fu, Zhang, & Li, 2014). This makes disaster risk management in various countries more complicated (O'Brien, O'Keefe, Rose, & Wisner, 2006), especially in poor regions and countries, which may cause even greater imbalances and inequality in development (Wisner & Walker, 2005) and will inevitably have a great impact on the education system, since educational opportunities are usually greatly restricted during a crisis (Wang, 2014). For example, vulnerable groups that have newly expanded due to the outbreak of the crisis may find it difficult to continue to obtain educational opportunities; schoolteachers and students may face physical safety or psychosocial risks on their way back to school or when they live at school. In view of the impact of severe disasters, building a national emergency response mechanism for the education system and the interaction of various subjects in the education emergency system have become urgent problems. Therefore, this book argues that in the face of a sudden crisis, various educational emergency measures under the leadership of the national government will help teachers and students affected by the crisis to deal calmly with their situation, and reduce the impact of the crisis on the rights of teachers and students. These measures would provide opportunities of carrying out online courses and guarantee the normal operation of the education system, and traditional education could even be changed, to produce a new mainstream form of education. For example, during the pandemic, GOC took the lead in issuing the "Postponed Start of School" and "Disrupted Classes, Undisrupted Learning" policy. Schools at all levels and various types have successively shifted to online education under the guidance of the policy, which provides opportunities for the rapid development of online education on a large scale. According to the statistics, as of March 17, 2020, there are as many as 440,000 pieces of information related to online education discussions, which has become a hot spot of public opinion (People's Network 2020a). Before February 5, 2020, for jointly implementing and guaranteeing online teaching in colleges and universities during the pandemic prevention and control period and to realize "stopping classes without stopping teaching and class without stopping school", the Ministry of Education issued instrument of "Guiding Opinions on Doing a Good Job in the Organization and Management of Online Teaching in General Institutions of Higher Education during the Period of Pandemic Prevention and Control", which required the government to take the lead based on universities, and the society to participate in the national online teaching activities. Since February 2, the Ministry of Education has organized 22 online course platforms to open more than 24,000 online courses for free, covering 18 disciplines in more than 12 undergraduate colleges and vocational colleges. On April 10, 2020, a video conference on the construction of an international platform for online teaching in Chinese universities, hosted by the Higher Education Department of the Ministry of Education, was held in Beijing. According to data from the conference, as of April 3, there were 1,454 regular colleges and universities nationwide online, and more than 950,000 teachers opened 942,000 and 7.133 million online courses, and 1.18 billion students participated in online courses (Chen, 2020). As the whole country began to respond to the call of the Ministry of Education for "Disrupted Class, Undisrupted Learning", primary and secondary schools as well as universities across the country were actively using various online platforms where enterprises provided free usage, which provided effective help for them to carry out online education. According to the requirements of the Ministry of Education, education department authorities at all levels, educational organizations, and enterprises should provide online learning resources and support services for teachers and students to ensure "Disrupted Class, Undisrupted Learning". After the outbreak of the pandemic, Chinese education enterprises provided a large number of high-quality online course resources and learning support services for free, and even added additional courses and services, such as family education and mental health education. While responding to the call of the country, this also helped their own development and won praise from many.

In this situation, online teaching does not simply mean putting instructional activities on a network platform. but rather doing a good job in the transformation of instructional methods and adopting distance education methods to carry out online education during the pandemic period, thus solving the problem of "at home" students. The state of "delayed learning" requires consideration of the transformation of the instructional organization structure, fluency of the instructional structure, diversity of the learning structure, and flexibility of the learning structure (Zhu & Peng, 2020). Accurate and flexible online and offline connection to teachers and students is the key to improving the ability of the education system to respond to disasters in the information era. This mainly starts from five aspects, which include: build a learner-oriented online curriculum system, consummate a quality-oriented online curriculum evaluation system, create a problem-oriented human-computer interaction curriculum ecology, choose the "whole body response" course implementation method, and construct a multi-subject collaborative education course environment, to attain a precise connection between online education and offline education (Liu, 2020a). During the pandemic, Chinese online education must first focus on optimizing a school's online education network environment and hardware equipment, to provide students with a personalized and diversified online education environment. This is the most difficult hardware problem in the transition from offline education to online education; Second, this is inseparable from the integration of high-quality online educational resources and management platforms, to ensure that online education resources and platforms are systematic, appropriate, and standardized (Fu, & Zhou, 2020). In short, the success of online education is closely related to the abundance of online education resources and platforms.

In addition, there were other foreseeable difficulties and challenges. Liu (2020c) argues that the most challenging thing is how to ensure that the quality of online classroom teaching is substantially equivalent to that of classroom teaching offline, where students and teachers do not have face-to-face communication. Zhu (2020) summarizes the possible problems: how to build a learning structure that suits local conditions; how to carry out learning at home; what to learn at home, and how to avoid excessively increasing the burden on students, parents, and teachers; what is the positioning of "Disrupted Class, Undisrupted Learning", and how to make connections after school starts. Additional issues include: how students learn effectively; how teachers carry out teaching; how the education department manages scientifically (Xu et al., 2020); how to ensure the efficiency of online learning at home for students, etc. Those are new tasks to be faced for every teacher (Zhou, 2020b). As online learning becomes the most important way of learning, various educational institutions must also develop teaching in new ways to solve various new professional, technical and management problems. If we can't solve these problems, it will greatly affect the quality of online education.

Online education under the pandemic has the potential for universality, inclusiveness, and participation, showing great advantages (Zhang, 2020b): (1) Not restricted by physical space, students can participate in learning at home, reducing the risk of spreading the pandemic; (2) Courses can be watched repeatedly, which provides allows students to review, summarize, and take notes; (3) High-quality teaching resources can be disseminated and sharied,in areas with lower education levels.. Therefore, online education can extend educational content and has excellent development prospects (Yang, 2020). But there are also many shortcomings: the number of online courses is huge, while the quality is uneven; students are required to have greater learning autonomy and self-discipline; more important, the lack of communication and interaction between teachers and students was not conducive to mobilizing students' enthusiasm for learning (Zhang, 2020a). To address these problems, online instruction can be optimized from different aspects, such as improving hardware facilities and software resources to provide a good environment for online teaching; changing the teaching concept from "teaching for teaching" to "teaching by learning"; innovating teacher training and research methods to improve teachers' online teaching design ability; and, using learning analysis technology to achieve data-driven teaching in accordance with their aptitude (Wang et al., 2020).

The call "Disrupted Class, Undisrupted Learning" proposed by the GOC was a major strategic opportunity to promote teaching reforms and carry out educational innovation. It was an important social practice for the development of all-staff education and comprehensive education, an important opportunity to improve education governance, and boosted the technological revolution (Liu, 2020b).

The scale, scope, and depth of online education at this time is an unprecedented initiative in the history of higher education in the world and the first such experiment on a global scale. It has not only successfully responded to the crisis of the suspension of schools, teaching, and classes brought about by the pandemic, but has also created a new peak of online teaching, explored new practices for online teaching, and formed a new paradigm for online teaching, with far-reaching significance for the future reform and development of higher education in China and around the world.

As more and more nations began to face the educational emergency from pandemics (e.g., avian flu or H1N1) or natural disasters (e.g., the Christchurch earthquakes), the availability of open online education is of critical importance (Tonk et al., 2013). Online learning could potentially continue education during school closures after disasters, offering students substantial benefits and learning opportunities, including the convenience of time and place. School administrators in earthquake-prone regions are called upon to develop emergency plans to deliver online learning, to mitigate the disruption of education delivery and the impacts on students and schools after disasters (Baytiyeh, 2018). In order to help students master the basic disaster management content, the government of Toronto, Canada, called on schools to develop, implement, and evaluate an online disaster management professional course from 2007 to 2008, including videos, forums, online table games, and virtual disaster simulations, which professionals participated in together (Atack et al., 2009). Promoting social cohesion through the improvement of the capabilities of school administrators with regard to shifting to an online teaching and learning mode during school dysfunctions or closures is key to the post-earthquake recovery of vulnerable communities in divided societies (Baytiyeh, 2019). One university in Taiwan has established an "earthquake school". Teachers educate students about earthquakes, and students also learn about earthquakes in an interesting environment (Liang et al., 2016).

In the United Kingdom, the Department of Higher Education and other departments have actively coordinated various colleges and universities to respond to the pandemic and suggested that all colleges and universities make corresponding educational model adjustments, in accordance with the government's prevention and control policy guidelines. With the spread of the pandemic in the UK, and a shortage of medical resources, teachers and students in British universities have begun to live at home. Many universities have started online teaching and examinations since March 16, 2020, and some have fully implemented online education, such as Imperial College London, the London School of Economics, King's College London, University College London, Durham University, Lanka University of Edinburgh, the University of Edinburgh, etc. (Zhao, 2020). The data shows that Zoom video conferencing software had 10 million active users at the end of 2020, and this number soared to more than 200 million in March 2020 (Yu, & Gui, 2020). In France, since March 16, most colleges and universities have stopped offline teaching and gradually begun online teaching, including École Polytechnique Paris, Grenoble École de Management, HEC Paris, the European School of Knowledge Economy and Management, the European Business School, etc. (Zhao, 2020).

In current studies of "educational emergency" and "emergency education", researchers are concerned with how to strengthen the government's handling of disasters and how to implement emergency education, to help students reduce the risk of disasters. Namely, integrating how to reduce the risk of disasters, and how to quickly return to normal life into the curriculum into contents. In contrast, fewer researchers pay attention to how multiple subjects in the education system should play their roles, how to take measures to reduce the impact of sudden disasters on the current development of the education system, and how the various subjects interact and play a role. From the existing literature, more will be combined with health education, or hygiene health education, etc. At the same time, online education is advocated as an emergency measure, to protect students' right to education and reduce the impact on teachers and students.

2 Theoretical basis

The sudden occurrence of disasters is likely to cause education systems to break down, then fail to operate normally. It is difficult to solve all problems if we rely on government alone. Therefore, it is necessary to seek new solutions and solutions from multiple subjects (Chen & Peng, 2020; Peng, 2020). The theory of welfare pluralism was proposed by scholars as an alternative to the welfare state after the crisis of the 1970s; it is also called a mixed economy of welfare. The theory emphasizes that the government is not the only provider of welfare, nor is the market, but rather the government, the market, and all parts of society jointly provide a diverse combination of welfare paradigms (Lin, 2002; Peng & Huang, 2006). According to the development process of welfare pluralism theory, there are two main schools of thought about the division of welfare providers: one is the triangle method, represented by Ross and others (Peng, 2015; Wang, 2010); the other is the quarter method, represented by Johnson and others (Tian & Zhong, 2009).

In 1986, Rose put forward a theory of multiple combinations of welfare. He argues that: (1) Social welfare comes from the three sectors of family, market, and country. Social welfare is a combination of these multiple elements, and the total amount of welfare is equal to the welfare produced in the family, plus the benefits obtained through market sales on the Internet and the benefits provided by the state. (2) Welfare is the product of the whole society, and no single subject can meet the needs of social welfare. Ross's thought breaks with the practice of welfare for the welfare state being provided entirely by the state, and established a basic analytic framework for diversified welfare supply (Tong & Zhang, 2018). In 1988, Evers described the diversity of Rose's welfare as a welfare unit composed of the family, the (market), economy and the country, namely the welfare triangle. He presents views similar to Ross's, and further develops Rose's views, proposing the research paradigm of the welfare triangle. On the basis of his comment on Rose's view of welfare pluralism, he advocates that the country, market, and family should be embodied in corresponding economic organizations, values, and social membership, and that the welfare triangle analysis framework should be discussed in the context of culture and politics. He argues that in the current "welfare diversification" policy, the emphasis is on collaboration, rather than on the mutual substitution of different departments.

DOI: 10.4324/9781003188261-2

Johnson (1999) is a typical representative of the quadrant. He divides welfare providers into four main bodies: the state, the market, the family, and the voluntary organization, and combines the voluntary organization based on the original three-part division of the state, the market, and the family. At the same time, he emphasizes that voluntary organizations, families, and other informal organizations play an important role in the process of providing welfare. Gilbert and Johnson present similar views. The difference is that Gilbert classifies the family as an informal organization and argues that social welfare comes from the government, the market, voluntary organizations, and informal organizations. The advanced nature of his ideas lies in realizing that these four subjects cannot be separated from each other; the four departments are interactive. In 1996, Eves further proposed the welfare quadrilateral analysis paradigm, arguing that social welfare comes from four aspects: the market, the state, the community, and civil society. In social welfare, civil society can make private and local interests basically consistent with public interests. At the same time, private capital is also of great significance to the integration of social welfare. Therefore, in the policy program of welfare pluralism, departments outside the government, such as the market, families, voluntary organizations, communities, and various mutual aid groups, play very important roles in the social welfare system (Li, 2017; Zhou & Tang, 2012).

In the present era, social welfare theory includes the diversity of welfare attitudes, group differences, and the correspondence between social welfare attitudes and the welfare system. Social welfare attitudes have changed from a system perspective to a risk perspective, becoming richer and more diverse (Shen & Lin, 2020). In China, the concept of an "appropriate universal-type social welfare system" has been formed, and social welfare development strategy has changed from negative to positive (Lin, 2015), which is reflected in the diversification of social welfare supply, the universalization of social welfare objects, and the systematization of social welfare content. In future, we will take the concept of a "better life" as the core idea of the social welfare system, and establish a state-leading social welfare system (Fan & Peng, 2019; Lin, 2019; Lin & Liang, 2019). Western countries have also developed from welfare states, to welfare pluralism, to welfare marketization. The welfare responsibilities of the government and citizens should be divided, and the responsibilities of the government, individuals, and the third sector should be clarified (Huang, 2000). The third sector plays the role of state contract agent in welfare supply. It should be a cooperative relationship with the government, not a competitive relationship (Han, 2012). The decentralization of government power and the privatization of social welfare should be emphasized (Lin & Wang, 2001), so as to promote the establishment of a new pattern of social assistance in which the government leads, social forces participate, and families and individuals also have the obligation to provide social assistance (Lin, 2020). Therefore, in education emergency management, the subjects that will be involved mainly include relevant United Nations agencies, international non-governmental organizations and domestic non-governmental organizations, or international institutions, educational organizations and related personnel, nongovernmental organizations, and civil organizations (Ding, 2012; Wu, 2010). Nongovernmental organizations and civil organizations are playing an increasingly important role and have become an important force in dealing with global problems and educational emergencies. Better linkage and coordination between different subjects requires the development and coordination of educational emergency objectives, better coordination of educational response capacity and educational evaluation, and better education emergency response initiatives, including curriculum, psychological assistance, resource allocation, and enhanced international collaboration (Liu & Zhou, 2012).

There have been more thorough theoretical studies on welfare pluralism at home and abroad, and the theoretical framework has been applied to practical problems, mainly to analyze social issues such as pensions, education, employment, social services, and social assistance (Li, 2012; Shi, 2016; Zhang, 2014). In this book, we mainly draw on Eves' quadrilateral welfare analysis paradigm, and analyze the government, enterprises, families, and schools as the four main subjects in this educational emergency.

The research on emergency management at home and abroad mainly focuses on emergency disasters. It is believed that the government lacks mature experience in handling emergency disasters, which will lead to large-scale uncontrollable property losses and casualties. Therefore, the government should strengthen emergency management, the public's emergency education, and emphasize the importance of emergency management, and then form a national emergency culture (Barnett et al., 2005; US Senate, 2006; Waugh, 2006), in which the Ego Effect of emergency responders will be positively related to the emergency resources and emergency preparation (Paeka & Hilyard, 2010).

In response to this, different scholars have divided emergency management into different stages. The common increments are three stages, four stages, five stages, and six stages. Generally, a stage is named for its management approach. For example, the three-stage model now has: (1) a. Early warning stage, b. disposal stage, c. recovery management (Hu, 2007). (2) a. Precrisis management stage (specifically early warning, prevention, disaster preparedness), b. crisis management stage (rapid response, emergency disposal), and c. postcrisis management stage (summary, evaluation, accountability) (Yin, 2009).

The four-phase model represents the four phases of emergency management and can also be considered as the four activities in emergency management (Zhao, 2014): (1) Reduction phase, preparation phase, reaction phase, recovery phase (Chen et al., 2011; Hou & Li, 2013; Robert et al., 2004). (2) Prediction phase, prevention phase, response phase, immunization phase (Wei, 1994). (3) Monitoring and early warning phase, pre-control and prevention phase, emergency treatment phase, assessment and recovery phase (Li, 2003). During the epidemic, Phil Hill proposed a four-stage model for the implementation of higher education. The first stage is a rapid transition to distance learning (February 2020–March 2020). The second stage is (re) Solid foundation (April 2020–July 2020), The third stage is the transition during continuous turbulence (August 2020–December 2020), and the fourth stage is the emergence of a new normal and new paradigms (2021 and beyond).

The five-stage model mainly includes: (1) Signal detection stage, preparation stage, prevention stage, loss control stage, and immunity stage (Mirtoff & Pearson, 1993); (2) Discovery stage, confirmation stage, analysis stage, evaluation stage, processing stage (Ryuzawa, 1999). The six-stage theory includes mainly the crisis prevention stage, crisis preparation stage, crisis confirmation stage, crisis control stage, crisis resolution stage, and learning stage (Norman, 2001).

As can be seen, different response measures should be taken at different stages after a crisis. Each subject is both a participant and a stakeholder. It should be ensured that under the leadership of the government, the education reconstruction work should be carried out, to form a joint force and at the same to ensure the effectiveness and transparency of the coordination. The establishment of independent institutions can be used to contact the government and other aid subjects, providing a carrier for communication between the two subjects (Wang, 2014). Therefore, in the face of a sudden crisis or epidemic, whether the linkage mechanism of the education system can mobilize the most extensive forces is an important criterion for evaluating whether the emergency mechanism is optimal. In emergency management, it is necessary to build an integrated education emergency mechanism of "early warning, hierarchical response, emergency iteration, and handling aftermath". At the same time, an emergency linkage mechanism should be established, that is led by governments at all levels and education administrative departments and other relevant departments of society (Zhao, 2010).

3 Research methods

3.1 The time nodes

In this research, three time-nodes (January 23, 2020, February 17, 2020, and March 1, 2020) have been set and studied. After the outbreak of COVID-19, the scope of stoppage and school suspension across the country continued to expand. In response to a call by the Ministry of Education, the education bureaus of all provinces and cities began to issue notices postponing the start of school, and then the Ministry of Education issued documents to implement the "Disrupted Class, Undisrupted Learning" policy. Therefore, the core problems faced by each subject in different periods and the four periods in which corresponding countermeasures were taken are divided according to time when official documents were issued by the Ministry of Education of China. Based on this, the development of online education during the whole process of educational emergence can be divided into four stages. First of all, on January 27, 2020, starting from the date when the Ministry of Education issued the notice of the extension of schools in the spring semester, we started to collect relevant information about the four subjects under "Disrupted Class, Undisrupted Learning". Then, on February 12, 2020, the General Office of Ministry of Education and the Ministry of Industry and Information issued the document "Deployment about Related Work in the Activitiy of 'Disrupted Class, Undisrupted Learning' in Primary and Secondary Schools". At this point, the period from January 27, 2020, to February 12, 2020, were divided into the first stage of the "Classes Suspended but Learning Continues". We defined this stage as the "proposal period" in the education emergency of "Massive Online Education". Subsequently, from February 13, 2020, to March 1, 2020 (the day before the official opening of most schools nationwide), the period was considered the second stage of the "Classes Suspended but Learning Continues" activity and defined as the "exploratory period" of the formal "Massive Online Education" education emergency plan. Later, on March 24, 2020, the General Office of the Ministry of Education and the General Office of the Ministry of Civil Affairs issued a notice proposing to make an overall plan for the resumption of classes. The civil affairs department and the education department were to cooperate with the schools to complete the preparatory work before the schools started.

DOI: 10.4324/9781003188261-3

Therefore, the period from March 2, 2020, to March 23, 2020, was divided into the third stage of the activity, which was the "fully deployed period" of the formal "Massive Online Education" education emergency plan. At the same time, the period after March 24, 2020 was defined as the fourth stage, called the "exit period" of the education emergency plan. During this period, people from all walks of life began to return to work in a wide range of activities, and correspondingly, more and more schools began to prepare for the opening date and the resumption of classes. Thus, the formal massive online education that took place before the fourth stage was gradually returning to traditional teaching at brick-and-mortar schools, a gradual transition back to face-to-face teaching. But this gradual transition process couldn't achieve a quick exit, that is, online education is still indispensable and will not be quickly suspended.

3.2 The targeted agents

The four independent subjects under the education emergency analyzed in this book constituted an education emergency ecosystem, and the four subjects were the core elements of this ecosystem. Each subject played its own role and interconnected with other subjects from different angles, at different levels, and in different depths, making the whole education emergency ecosystem present a dynamic state of circulation. By analyzing the problems faced by the three subjects under the policy guidance of the Chinese government during the epidemic, and the countermeasures adopted by the government, this study aims to provide some reference of experience for other countries.

Based on the theory of welfare pluralism, this study selected four subjects, namely the government, school, family, and enterprise, and three elements, namely teachers, students and parents, as its analytic objects.

The study analyzed government policies in the four periods of the "Classes Suspended but Learning Continues" activity, and then discussed the schools, enterprises, and families under the policy background, as well as conducting random sampling of relevant posts. The research objects were mainly in four categories:

(1) Government: Including the Ministry of National Education and the State Council, as well as local and municipal governments and education bureaus.
(2) Schools: All kinds of schools at the provincial and municipal levels.
(3) Enterprises: The enterprises providing educational products.
(4) Families: Students and parents participating in the "Classes Suspended but Learning Continues" activities.

As is known to all, in the major educational emergence events, the leading role was often played by the government and various educational administrative departments at all levels, especially the various leading policies and documents issued by them, which could play an important role in guiding, supporting, and leading other subjects in the education ecosystem. Apart from the role and status of the "commander" of the government departments, the two subjects that played a practical, defensive, and responsive role in a series of major education emergency events were usually the schools and families, and they crossed and integrated the core elements of the whole education ecosystem: teachers and students. Due to the special period of the epidemic, a large area of work stoppage has been caused. Therefore, parents also played a crucial role in the process of students' online education at home, which was a significant bridge for home-school cooperation.

In addition, given the huge range, sudden outbreak, and the irreversible negative damage and loss, the enterprises with rich social resources, talent resources, and educational resources, not only took the lead in changes within the business model, but also adjusted the majority of teaching resources for online education. Adhering to the selfless spirit of serving the society, teachers, and students, enterprises greatly promoted the development of the largest scale of formal online education in history and provided convenient conditions and resources for its development. It could be said that in the whole process of the "Massive Formal Online Education" education emergency plan, enterprises played a crucial role as "Leader", "Supporter," and "Rear Camp". Therefore, the four subjects previously mentioned were selected as the objects of analysis in this study.

3.3 Data collection

This book mainly adopted content analysis to collect data. Full and objective data is the foundation of grounded theory; considering the purpose of this study and the actual maneuverability, this study used the content analysis method to collect and analyze the governments' policy documents, general web information from major search engines, WeChat public articles, the discussion thread of knowledge-sharing platforms of a social nature, such as Weibo and Zhihu, and other data from multiple channels.

The main data collection channels in this study were as follows:

(1) Major search engines, such as 360SE, Baidu SE, Bing SE, and so on.
(2) Education websites, such as China Education News Web, Xinhua Net, Guangming Net, China Education Daily, and so on.
(3) WeChat official accounts (the WeChat official accounts of various schools, units, and the official education department of provinces and cities).
(4) Education websites of the Chinese Ministry of Education, provincial and municipal departments.
(5) Social networking platforms, such as Zhihu, Weibo, etc.

In this study, data retrieval was conducted in four different periods, as mentioned earlier, and the specific methods were as follows:

(1) The main search channels of the government were the official websites of the Ministry of Education, provincial and municipal education departments, and the official WeChat official accounts of the provincial and municipal education departments, etc.
(2) The main search channels of the schools were related education websites, such as China Education News Web, Xinhua Net, Guangming Net, China Education Daily, and WeChat official accounts (the WeChat official accounts of various schools, units, and the official education departments of provinces and cities).
(3) The main search channels of enterprises were mainly several mainstream search engines, including Baidu SE, 360 SE, Bing SE, and WeChat official accounts (the WeChat official accounts of enterprises or organizations).
(4) The main search channels for families included Zhihu, Weibo, Tik Tok, and WeChat official accounts, etc.

After retrieving results, the authors first quickly read through the full text. If it had no obvious problems involving or countermeasures to the "Classes Suspended but Learning Continues" activity during COVID 19 outbreaks, the authors deleted the data. However, if the data was related to the problems confronted by the subjects under the epidemic situation and the education emergency countermeasure adopted, then they kept the data. At the same time, the core text content of the data was extracted separately for archiving, in order to analyze and encode the text content. The amount of data collected by the four subjects in each stage is shown in Table 3.1. After archiving the data of the four subjects according to the date of the four periods, then the coding process go to the coding link of the data.

3.4 The coding scheme

This research adopted the grounded theory method, selected the documentary data of "the problems faced by the government, schools, enterprises and families and their countermeasures under the outbreak of COVID-19" as the research objects, and conducted content analysis and coding based on a large amount of qualitative text data. Grounded theory is a kind of qualitative

Table 3.1 The amount of data collected by the four subjects in the four periods

Periods/Subjects	Governments	Schools	Enterprises	Families
Proposal period	31	105	102	30
Exploratory period	30	117	120	30
Fully deployed period	30	165	111	60
Exit period	31	203	149	40

research method rooted in the actual materials, which uses systematic procedures to inductively guide the research process, aiming at a certain phenomenon (Chen, 2020). It adopts the bottom-up method, based on the collection and analysis of various data, refining the core concepts that reflect the content of the data, and then establishes the relationship between these concepts, so as to construct the theory (Strauss, 1987). The authors' method embodied two main characteristics: the first was a systematic research procedure; the second was to use the induction method for analysis. These two characteristics were mainly reflected in the key element of the qualitative data analysis, the three-level coding process. This process usually extracted concepts from the description of the original data (first-level coding), then classified the description to obtain the category (second-level coding), and finally established connections between the classifications, to obtain the concept network (third-level coding).

In order to ensure the reliability and representativeness of the samples, except for government documents, the selection of other samples was determined according to the page views displayed in the system, that is, the materials reported by mainstream media, read by a large number of people, and receiving a high rate of replies would be given priority. In order to ensure the reliability and validity of coding results, the research adopted a triangular cross-verification method. The accuracy and reliability of the research was guaranteed through mutual support by and cross-comparison of data from government files, network platforms, WeChat, and forum posts. In addition, the research adopted the method of co-coding by two researchers, and expert guidance, to ensure the effectiveness of coding.

The two researchers coded independently of each other. The coding process is as follows:

(1) Extract concept from raw data description.
    The two researchers read the data of the four subjects in the four periods, respectively, and preliminarily sorted out and summarized the subjects of the data: the problems they faced (core problems and subproblems) and the solutions they pursued (core solutions and sub-solutions), so as to form the first-level coding.
(2) On the basis of the first-level coding, the concepts extracted were classified, to obtain the category.
    The problems and countermeasures confronted by the single subject in the four periods were extracted, and the similarities were merged. The merging conditions were as follows: Each core problem was a parallel relationship and contained the corresponding subproblems, and the subproblems were also a parallel relationship. Similarly, the core countermeasures were the same. After that, the data copies of each problem and countermeasure in a single subject under the three periods were counted, and the second-level coding with the classification category was finally formed.

(3) The conceptual network was obtained by establishing the relationship between classifications on the basis of the second-level coding.

The complete framework was sorted out, and the problems faced by the four subjects (government, schools, enterprises, and families) and the counter-measures taken in the four periods were presented in the form of tables. The conceptual network was obtained through the connection and interaction between the classification problems and countermeasures of the four sub-jects' second-level coding, and the third-level coding was finally formed.

This chapter briefly introduced the principle and process of coding by tak-ing the government, in the first stage, as an example. The two researchers jointly analyzed the summary of the phenomenon of the original policies (31), encoded as A1-A31, and further normalized it to obtain 120 (zz1-zz120) initial concepts. It could be seen that the initial concepts were mostly repeti-tive, so the initial concepts needed to be merged; finally, we received 47 initial concepts, coding for Z1-Z47. For example: Network course teaching, the development and education activities related to COVID-19, adjust the teach-ing arrangement as a whole, the teachers immediately help students with feedback, avoid unnecessary increasing burden of students, focus on stu-dents' vision, a reasonable arrangement of students' schedule, strengthen students' psychological counsel, related enterprises provide network techni-cal support and guide the parents to control children's electronic products using time, etc. According to the correlation and correlation degrees between the initial concepts, the concepts were further categorized, that is, they were reclassified and combined, and finally a total of 21 categories were obtained, which were numbered ZZ1-ZZ21, such as the deployment of "Disrupted Class, Undisrupted Learning" preparatory work, the overall arrangement of teachers' online teaching work, online learning and support services for teachers and students, strengthened parent-school collaboration, supporting teachers' training cooperation to promote informational teaching, and encouraging teachers to use effective teaching methods and perfect teaching online monitoring mechanisms to ensure the quality of teaching.

The collaborative coding process of the two researchers was mainly as follows:

(1) Horizontally and vertically compare the carding results for the same data.
(2) Communicate and discuss the existing categories of differences.
(3) Obtain consistent conclusions on the problems and countermeasures presented in the data, to form the final category representation.
(4) Repeat the preceding verification steps until all the data for a certain subject under a certain stage has been verified.
(5) Repeat the preceding verification steps until all the data have been verified.

Finally, SPSS was used to calculate the Kappa coefficient of the coding results. This result indicated that the internal consistency of the two researchers' coding results was satisfactory and could be used for subsequent analysis. In order to facilitate the review, based on the aforementioned coding, this book presents the main problems faced by the three subjects (schools, enterprises, and families) in four periods in the form of a table and briefly describes the countermeasures.

3.5 The coding process

In order to abstract and conceptualize the original data (government files, network platform data, WeChat data, and forum post data) according to the grounded theory method, the research first carried out open coding. In consideration of semantic integrity, the research adopted sentence-by-sentence coding. Considering the large number of data collection channels, for the convenience of the analysis, the researchers divided all data into four categories based on different subjects: the letters "G" (government), "S" (school), "E" (enterprise), and "F" (family) were marked before the coding content to indicate the difference, and "Ga", "Gb", "Gc", "Gd", "Sa", "Sb", "Sc", "Sd", "Ea", "Eb", "Ec", "Ed", "Fa", "Fb", "Fc", and "Fd" were further marked for each corresponding period. Data for every subject in each period was encoded in three rounds, as open coding, axial coding, and selective coding:

(1) Open coding
Through a summary of the phenomenon and further normalization of the original comment statements encoded as Ga1-Ga240, a total of 300(zz1-zz300) initial concepts were obtained. As these initial concepts were numerous and highly repetitive, it was necessary to classify and merge them, and thus a total of 47 initial concepts were obtained, encoded as Z1-Z47. According to the different degrees of extraction, open coding can be divided into initial coding, labeling, and initial conceptualization.

(2) Axial coding
The concepts obtained from open coding were classified, compared, and categorized, and the "main category" was extracted to determine the category code, so as to establish the relationships between different levels of coding.

(3) Selective coding
Determined all the core categories under each subject and the relationship between all levels of coding, and built the linkage model of the four subjects of the system.

Considering the extensive content of the three-round coding, for the purpose of reducing the space occupied, the main body of this book only presents the

Table 3.2 Examples of open coding and axial coding of policy

Coding Number	Original Statement	Conceptualization	Category
Ga1	If possible, schools should actively explore the "Internet +" mode to carry out distance education teaching activities and online learning courses, and the "Zhijianghui" education plaza will continue to open and provide high-quality online learning resources for basic education.	Z1: Provide qualified online learning resources for basic education free of charge. Z2: Develop distance education teaching activities and online learning courses.	ZZ1: Deploy the "Disrupted Class, Undisrupted Learning" preparation work. ZZ2: Provide technical resources for a wide range of "Disrupted Class, Undisrupted Learning" activities.
Ga2	In principle, the schools used their own mature digital platforms and existing online resources or constructional courses to carry out teaching work. Extensive collection of enterprises (industries) online teaching resources for job training, as supplementary teaching materials for schools' teaching. Give full play to the leading role of "Extra High Plan" constructional schools among the vocational schools, gather outstanding teachers at related vocational schools and experts from enterprises to jointly develop and produce high-quality courses, and open up high-quality intercollegiate network teaching and network sharing practical training resources. Teachers of all courses should adjust the course syllabus soundly, make effective connection with offline teaching after the resumption of schools, arrange teaching time flexibly, and organize students to carry out theoretical teaching through network independent learning, mixed teaching, live teaching, online assessment, and other methods. Teaching staff should notify every single student about the adjusted teaching arrangement through WeChat groups, QQ groups, or other ways, and do an organized job of supervision and evaluation, to ensure the quality of network teaching.	Z3: Select mature teaching platforms and decent teaching resources. Z4: The teachers should adjust the curriculum soundly. Z5: Organize students to choose appropriate learning styles. Z6: Do an organized job in teaching supervision and evaluation to ensure the quality of network teaching.	ZZ3: Encourage teachers to adopt effective teaching methods. ZZ4: Improve the online teaching monitoring mechanism to ensure the quality of teaching. ZZ5: Pay attention to the problems of students' network learning burden.
Ga3	Online MOOCs and high-quality online course teaching resources at the provincial and university levels are utilized, to actively carry out online teaching and learning activities under the support of MOOCs and experimental resource platforms, so as to ensure teaching progress and quality during the epidemic prevention and control period. Increase students' independent learning time, strengthen the online learning process and the quality of multiple assessment requirements	Z7: Make full use of qualified online teaching resources and platforms. Z8: Actively carry out online teaching activities. Z9: Increase students' independent study time.	ZZ6: Attach importance to physical and mental health issues.

core problems faced by each subject in the four periods of the three-round coding and the percentage results. Combined with the coding method of the government in the first stage – the proposal period in the coding scheme – three rounds of coding were carried out, as open coding, axial coding, and selective coding. The coding results are partially shown in Table 3.2, with further details in Table A1 of Appendix A.

In order to find the relationships between the initial concepts and the category, and determine the major and minor categories, qualitative and quantitative methods were used to carry out axial coding, and the percentage of each initial concept in the total number of samples was calculated, as shown in Table A2 of Appendix A. Through the overall data analysis in Table A2 of Appendix A, initial concepts that accounted for less than 20% were eliminated or integrated. Thus, the coding table for the government, containing 21 countermeasures, was finally obtained, as shown in Table A3 of Appendix A.

As mentioned earlier, the research mainly divided the timeline into four periods, to analyze the coding, problems, and countermeasures for three subjects, namely schools, families, and enterprises, under the guidance of policy. The coding process also followed the coding method of the government subject in the first stage – the proposal period – and carried out three rounds of coding, as open coding, axial coding, and selective coding. The complete coding process of the first stage is shown in Appendix A, and the complete coding process of the other three stages is shown in Appendices B, C, and D, respectively. Specifically:

(1) For the government, we mainly analyzed the release trend and specific guidance of the policy adjustment related to "COVID-19".
(2) For schools, we mainly analyzed the core problems faced by schools and the effective core countermeasures taken by schools in different stages, such as changing the traditional brick-and-mortar classroom education to large-scale formal online education, gradually withdrawing online education, and returning to face-to-face education in schools under the guidance of government's policy.
(3) For enterprises, we analyzed the core problems and measures faced by enterprises, especially educational enterprises, in the process of adjusting their offline education industry and responding to and taking practical actions to support the adjustment of the online education emergency plan under the guidance of the government.
(4) For families, we mainly analyzed the core problems they faced in the process of responding to and taking practical actions to support the "home-based" online education, as well as their countermeasures.

On this basis, the book also analyzes teachers, students, and parents, and finally summarizes and sorts out the changes in the four subjects' actions in the education emergency ecosystem and the linkage relationships between them, as shown as shown in Figure 3.1.

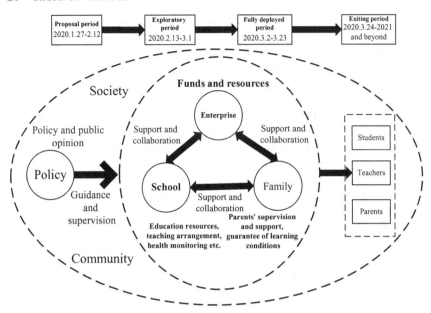

Figure 3.1 The changes in action of the four subjects in the four stages, and the relationships connecting them.

4 The first stage

Proposal period

4.1 The policy orientation of government

Under the government's education emergency plan, "Disrupted Class, Undisrupted Learning", the Ministry of Education and provincial and municipal education departments provided the key institutions in the education emergency ecosystem, which mainly made requirements and guidelines for the overall deployment of the extension of school opening from the four dimensions of educational departments, schools, teachers, and families. During the proposal period of the "Disrupted Class, Undisrupted Learning" campaign, the government's main policy orientation was as shown in Table A3 of Appendix A.

As the subject in the whole education ecosystem, in the beginning of the proposal of "Disrupted Class, Undisrupted Learning", the government provided guidance to schools, enterprises, and families and also set relevant requirements.

4.1.1 Schools

At the organizations' level: The government set relevant requirements for local education departments, creating emergency measures and deployment arrangements for education, including delaying the opening of schools, grasping the overall requirements of teaching, overall planning, building a high-quality network teaching resource library and free network teaching platform, and requiring relevant departments and enterprises to provide network technology support. It also emphasized the public welfare of the relevant curriculum resources.

At the teachers' level: The government provided relevant policy guidance to all kinds of schools at all levels to carry out "Disrupted Class, Undisrupted Learning". The specific requirements included carrying out education activities related to the pandemic situation, supporting teachers' training and cooperation, and providing the guidance and requirements for teachers who carry out network teaching, including improving their own information-based

DOI: 10.4324/9781003188261-4

teaching level, adopting effective teaching methods, providing help and feed-back to students immediately, guiding parents to do a good job in family education, and so on.

At the students' level: Attention should be paid to the burden of students' online learning, the cultivation of students' autonomous learning ability, students' physical and mental health, and home–school cooperation.

4.1.2 Enterprises

At the organizations' level: The government encouraged enterprises to provide technical resources support for the smooth implementation of the large-scale "Disrupted Class, Undisrupted Learning" activity and encouraged them to adhere to the public welfare of online courses and online teaching resources.

At the teachers' level: It is recommended that enterprises could provide information-based training for teachers together with schools. At the student level, it could provide students with high-quality learning resources and the use of webcast platforms as an auxiliary tool for online learning.

At the families' level: Parents could be guided to master the methods of online learning, to tutor younger students in carrying out online learning.

4.1.3 Family

The government provided relevant guidance and suggestions for students' online learning at home, such as adding knowledge of pandemic prevention and control into daily courses, strengthening online interaction with teachers, choosing an appropriate way to learn and study independently, etc., which were to guide and regulate students' home study. At the same time, it also provided relevant suggestions and guidance for parents who participated in the activity of "Disrupted Class, Undisrupted Learning" to accompany young students in e-learning, including learning efficiency, vision health, technical operation, and other issues.

In general, the government took the lead in advancing the call of "Disrupted Class, Undisrupted Learning", and meanwhile, it began to guide other subjects to gradually explore and actively cooperate with the comprehensive implementation of this activity. It reflected the leading role of the government in the education and teaching ecosystem and provided a standard for other subjects of "Disrupted Class, Undisrupted Learning" within their respective coordination scope.

4.2 The policy-oriented actions of schools, families, and enterprises

After the completion of the coding, the main problems faced by the three subjects, namely schools, families, and enterprises are shown in the Table 4.1, in view of the documents of "Delay the Start of School" and "Disrupted Class, Undisrupted Learning" put forward by the government in the initial stage.

To overcome the aforementioned problems, the main countermeasures taken by the schools, families, and enterprises are as follows:

4.2.1 Schools

At the organizations' level: Schools made emergency education measures and corresponding arrangements, and prepared for the delayed opening of the schools. For example, the schools organized leaders, experts, and teachers to set up an expert inspection group for pandemic prevention and control, and formulated various pandemic prevention plans and teaching adjustment plans under "Disrupted Class, Undisrupted Learning", including monitoring the physical and mental health and safety of teachers and students, adjusting teaching programs to online education, delaying the opening time, and communicating timely with teachers and parents during the deployment of

Table 4.1 The difficulties encountered by schools, families, and enterprises in the proposal period

Subject	Difficulties Encountered		Proportion (%)
Schools	Organizations' Level	Deploy the problem of delaying the opening of schools to fight against COVID-19	74.28
		How to coordinate teachers' teaching work	60.00
		Problems in providing online learning support services for teachers and students	57.14
	Teachers' Level	Problems in implementing online teaching	80.00
		Provide learning support services for students in online education	68.57
		Face the challenge of online education in the course of suspension	34.29
		Test students' online teaching effect	25.71
		Timely monitoring and feedback of students' health	28.57
	Students' Level	Let students accept and carry out the problems of suspension of classes	25.71
		Reducing the impact of online education on students' eyesight	20.00

Subject	Difficulties Encountered		Proportion (%)
Families	Students' Level	Learning efficiency	26.98
		Students' poor autonomous learning ability	11.11
		Students' unfamiliarity to the way of taking classes	7.94
		Lack of autonomous learning time	7.94
		Students' poor attention to their study	4.76
	Parents' Level	Uncertainty of weather the college entrance examination and senior high school entrance examination postponed or not	33.33
		The increasing burdens on parents	30.16
		Communication and cooperation between Family and School	11.11
		Students' poor learning effect	50.79
		Vision and hearing health problems	20.63
	Objective Level	Teachers lacked information-based teaching training	20.63
		Network equipment technology would be stuck	17.46
		Lack of interaction between teachers and students	17.46
		Lack of rich extracurricular activities	17.46
		Teachers couldn't pay full attention to all the students	14.29
		Lack of network learning equipment	11.11
		Lack of teaching materials	11.11
		Problems related to learning environment	11.11
		The unclear learning tasks	11.11

Subject	Difficulties Encountered		Proportion (%)
Enterprises	Organizations' Level	The problem of providing resource support for a wide range of suspension	100.00
	Teachers' Level	Provide online teaching support services for front-line teachers	79.41
	Students' Level	The problem of providing online learning support services for students	67.65
	Families' Level	Provide online learning resources and support services for families and parents	45.50

relevant work, through trial and screening. Schools would select the appropriate teaching platform and online resources for themselves.

At the same time, in a timely manner, all schools needed to follow the guidance of the higher education departments and introduce the relevant plans for the implementation of online teaching. The teaching process was shifted from offline to online, and arrangements were made for teachers' teaching work as a whole. It was emphasized that teachers' online teaching should show a high sense of responsibility and carry out teaching effectively. The schools endeavored to transfer the large-scale face-to-face teaching of the classroom to online teaching, which was required the schools pay close attention to the guidance of teachers and provide all kinds of teaching support services, including guiding teachers to actively change fixed face-to-face teaching concepts, ideas, and methods. According to the actual needs of online education, schools could make relevant adjustments to re-face the new online teaching methods and implement teaching objectives. Moreover, they could provide a variety of support services, including organizing teachers and calling on them to participate in a series of training sessions and workshops for designing and developing online teaching resource and other training work. In order to improve teachers' ability to use information technology, which would benefit online education, the schools provided teachers with educational information expert, provided sufficient teaching resources and tools, guided teachers to constantly explore and reflect on the summary in the online teaching practice, and adjusted teaching as a result of interactive feedback with students.

At the teachers' level: The schools guided teachers in preparing to get teaching done. It was necessary to investigate the network environment of students in advance, because the network conditions of different places were different. This was also one of the key factors for the smooth development of online teaching. Simultaneously, the two levels of educational administration departments needed to act in a unified way, work in a division of labor and cooperation, and carry out activities at all levels. Moreover, teachers needed to have a general understanding of the class. The communication between teachers and students needed to be competent. At this time, teachers should be actively guided to be familiar with the relevant functions of the teaching platform selected by online teaching in advance, so as to ensure its smooth use in teaching, set an example for students, and urge them to be familiar with the online teaching platform. In order to ensure the effectiveness and diversity of students' online learning, teachers also needed to provide diversified learning resources. It was stipulated that teachers should carry out online course construction in advance according to the arranged courses, improve the curriculum syllabus, rearrange their teaching plan, perfect the exercise library, answer questions online, and set up an assessment and performance evaluation scheme. It was also emphasized that teachers must conform to the actual situation of online teaching in course construction and be encouraged to update their teaching methods.

On the students' level: The schools should timely check the health status of the students and arrange for the corresponding responsible teachers to collect and monitor the health information of the students every day, to remind the relevant students of the seriousness of the pandemic, and provide timely feedback to the schools. Schools ought to strive to develop or provide high-quality education resource platforms and online teaching platforms and organize the participation of teachers and students in an organized and effective way. Meanwhile, schools should take positive psychology as guidance, exploit students' positive personality and potential advantages, increase students' positive emotional experience, build a supportive organization and psychological environment, stimulate students' interest in online learning, and let students accept online learning fundamentally. The long-term online learning during the pandemic has a certain impact on students' eyesight, so students should be aware of the need to protect their eyesight. In addition, schools should try to explain the relevant precautions, including the learning posture, the choice of light while learning, the placement of electronic products, etc., and require teachers to remind students regularly. At the same time, schools should scientifically limit the time of online learning and guide students to do eye exercises, so that students can learn online healthily, effectively, and scientifically.

In general, in the proposal period, the schools responded actively to the documents of "Disrupted Class, Undisrupted Learning" and "Postponement of Schools' Opening" called for by the Chinese Ministry of Education. However, the documents were only commands, there too few clear measures, and the schools couldn't simply rely on the organization of experts, for most of the schools couldn't organize the experts who discussed and explored various possible online education programs under the wave of large-scale online education according to the actual conditions of the school to digest and understand "Disrupted Class, Undisrupted Learning", so as to ensure that the teachers and students of the whole school could really achieve Classes Suspended but Learning Continues. Therefore, at this time, the schools mainly accepted the current situation of the large-scale suspension of classes in the whole society and the education emergency call of turning face-to-face teaching into online teaching, actively carried out teaching activities in the passive situation, undertook the teaching deployment related to pandemic prevention and control, and guided teachers and students to face the practical needs and challenges of online education, todo a good job in the psychological construction of online education and provide support and services for teachers and students.

4.2.2 Families

In the early days of the proposal of "Disrupted Class, Undisrupted Learning", the family was the main subject of the whole education ecosystem, which confronted the main problems. The countermeasures proposed by the government, schools, and enterprises were to serve the families and solve the problems encountered by the families, in a certain sense. In the first stage of the proposal period, the families collected the problems around the three dimensions of "Students' level", "Parents' level", and "Objective level" in the activity of "Disrupted Class, Undisrupted Learning". Among them, the proportion of objective problems was the largest. To a certain extent, it showed that the activity of "Disrupted Class, Undisrupted Learning" was more "No Support" than "Support" in the whole audience at the beginning, which indicated that the large-scale use of the whole distance network for education was relatively not accepted by the public. Therefore, in the early stage, the families were confronting problems, whether at the students', parents', or objective level, and there were almost no countermeasures for the subject itself.

4.2.3 Enterprises

During the outbreak of the pandemic, enterprises that originally wired education courses and related products were in the "Internet plus education" field, especially in educational institutions (most of the enterprises gathered in this study were also enterprises or educational institutions). They were keen to catch up with the possibility of failing to carry out off-line classroom teaching on schedule, and actively adjusted to online education. Enterprises and educational institutions with online education products should increase the input and output of online education, scientifically adjust and deploy new online education programs and educational products, and ensure that the quality of products and services will receive a bad impact as little as possible, which were caused by the inconsistency with basic teaching and learning rules. The characteristics of the enterprises, that was to say, the profit-oriented nature of non-school subjects, determined that they hardly needed to directly participate in the process of teaching and learning. Therefore, compared with other subjects, the problems the enterprises faced were relatively singular, divided into the enterprises' organizational level, the frontline teachers' level, the students' level, and the families' level, so the corresponding questions were "What could the enterprises do for the suspension of classes?", "What kind of teaching support services can the enterprises provide to frontline teachers?", "What kind of learning support services can they provide to students?", and "What online learning resources and support services can be provided for parents?" Each problem also corresponded to a relatively clear solution. The enterprises mainly adopted the following countermeasures for these four aspects of the problem:

(1) **At the organizations' level**: For technical support under the policy of "Disrupted Class, Undisrupted Learning", enterprises actively provided a great deal of free online education support and services for all kinds of schools at all levels, including online education platforms and function instructions, education products, curriculum resources, other teaching resources, and teaching tools. Some enterprises even personalized online teaching programs for schools, actively responded to the policy of "Disrupted Class, Undisrupted Learning", and effectively solved the problems of teaching software operation and online classroom design faced by the large-scale use of online teaching activities all over the country. In the process, enterprises faced the problems of how to design the functions of urging students to learn before and after class, when developing teaching tools, such as a preview before class, timely feedback after class, and so on.

(2) **At the teachers' level**: For the problem of providing online teaching technology services to frontline teachers, some enterprises assigned special technical support personnel to schools, which provided ongoing teacher training support and assistance, and operation instructions or commentary videos, so as to solve the problem that some older teachers found it difficult to use or operate the software.

(3) **At the students' level**: For the problem of providing online learning support services for students, considering the computer literacy of different students and other factors, enterprises tried their best to make tools easy to operate, and resources easy to find and store in the development and design stage, and offered students instructional support.

(4) **At the families' level**: For the problem of providing support services for different families, the enterprises also provided family courses for parents and students, so that parents could understand and master the needed communication skills with their children during the pandemic and maintain a warm atmosphere in the family under a tense external social environment. In the process, for the economic conditions of different families, enterprises needed to consider the high adaptability of resources and the convenience of local storage when developing teaching resources, so as to facilitate online learning in different network and configuration environments.

To sum up, when the Ministry of Education proposed that all teaching activities should be transferred to large-scale online education activities during the pandemic, enterprises could respond quickly and positively due to their own freedom, flexibility, and abundant resources, and their development was less affected during this stage.

4.3 The policy-oriented interaction of schools, enterprises, and families

After the government issued the policy "Disrupted Class, Undisrupted Learning" and "Extension of Schools", enterprises quickly made the switch in teaching mode, actively changed the form of teaching from offline education to online education, and developed education products to provide online education platforms, curriculum resources, other teaching resources, and teaching tools for teachers and students. With the positive investment of enterprises, the schools also adjusted the teaching plan, mobilized teachers to become familiar with online teaching methods as soon as possible, supervised the physical and mental health of teachers and students, and cared for teachers and students, especially those whose families were affected during the pandemic. Simultaneously, parents tried their best to provide children with decent learning conditions at home. They supervised their children's self-directed learning and exercise at home, and cared for their children's mental health. In the first stage, the score of the positive degree of the actions taken by each subject is: Enterprises > Schools > Families, which indicated that the Enterprises under the policy guidance in the first stage was the most active in taking action, followed by the school, which belonged to the good level, and the family was the least active, which was in the general level. The specific interaction is shown in Figure 4.1.

During the pandemic, the government promulgated the policies "Disrupted Class, Undisrupted Learning" and "Extension of Schools". Under the guidance of policy and public opinion, enterprises, schools, and families positively participated in the development of online learning:

(1) **The enterprises** mainly provided funds, online education resources, online education programs, product development and improvement, and technology training for teachers. Their object was mainly the school, and their connection with the family was relatively weak.
(2) **The schools** began to arrange the work of delaying the start of schools and adjusting the plan for online education. They prepared online education resources and cooperated with families to educate students. They were at the center of implementing online learning and had close contact with families and enterprises.
(3) **The families** were mainly to provide the conditions for home online learning and supervise children's home learning and sports. In addition, they supported the school work and so on. The work done by the family was to protect and support online education; however, the family's connection with enterprise was relatively weak. Students, teachers, and parents were the main participants in online learning. The cooperation of enterprises and families provided the basic conditions and guarantee, so that schools could carry out online learning on schedule and effectively.

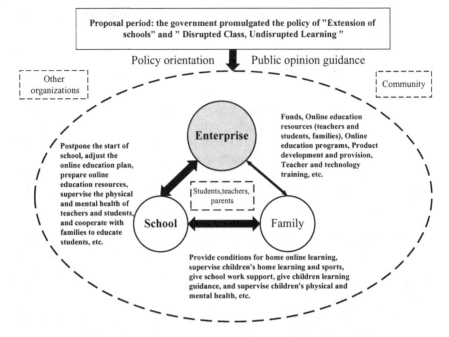

Figure 4.1 Interactive relationship chart of the three main subjects under the guidance of policy in the proposal period

5   The second stage

Exploratory period

5.1 The policy orientation of the government subject

After the "Disrupted Class, Undisrupted Learning" activity entered the exploratory period, on the basis of the basic policies advanced in the first stage, the government continued to provide supplementary guidance on the policies around the "Disrupted Class, Undisrupted Learning" activity first launched by some provinces and cities, combined with the schools, enterprises, and families, as shown in Table B3 of Appendix B.

In the exploratory period of "Disrupted Class, Undisrupted Learning", the government was still the main subject of the whole education ecosystem. Combined with the gradual progress of online curriculum activities across the country, it was suggested to continue to advance correspondingly more specific policy guidance for the deployment and requirements of the schools, enterprises, and families.

After a proposal period and an exploratory period, the government basically formed a relatively complete set of policy-oriented "Disrupted Class, Undisrupted Learning" activities.

5.2 The policy-oriented actions of schools, families, and enterprises

Under the policy guidance of the second stage, the main problems faced by the schools, families, and enterprises were as shown in Table 5.1.

To overcome these problems, the main countermeasures taken by the schools, families, and enterprises were as follows:

5.2.1 Schools

At the organizations' level: In the previous first stage, the schools were only making an initial response to the call. Through learning from the excellent experience of other schools, other provinces and cities, or the guidance and suggestions given by experts, they were trying to explore an effective implementation scheme of online education and teaching that was more in line with the actual conditions of the schools. At this time, the problems they

DOI: 10.4324/9781003188261-5

Table 5.1 The difficulties encountered by schools, families, and enterprises in the exploratory period

Subject	Difficulties Encountered		Proportion (%)
Schools	Organizations' Level	Problems in providing online learning support services for teachers and students	66.67
		The problem of rearrangement and adjustment of course content	64.10
		The problem of providing services to society	35.90
		The problem of overall planning and promoting teachers' teaching work	28.21
		Deployment of "Disrupted Class, Undisrupted Learning" and "Extension of schools".	23.08
	Teachers' level	Problems in implementing online teaching	69.23
		Provide learning support services for students in online education	66.67
		The challenge of online education in the course of suspension	41.03
		The effective evaluation of students' online teaching effect	38.46
	Students' Level	The problem of reducing the impact of online education on students' eyesight	47.22
		Timely monitoring and feedback of students' health	38.46
		Let students accept and carry out the problem of suspension of classes	5.13
	Students' Level	Learning efficiency	30.30
		Students' poor autonomous learning ability	16.67
		Students' unfamiliarity to the way of class	7.58
		Students' negative learning attitude	7.58

(*Continued*)

Subject	Difficulties Encountered		Proportion (%)
Families	Parents' Level	Increase the burden on parents	74.24
		Uncertainty about the date of the college entrance examination and senior high school entrance examination	33.33
		Parents' unfamiliarity with the use of related teaching platforms	7.58
		Communication and cooperation between families and schools	7.58
	Objective Level	The problem of network equipment technology stuck	66.67
		Students' poor learning effect	24.24
		Teachers lacked of information-based teaching training	21.21
		Problems related to learning environment	16.67
		Lack of interaction between teachers and students	16.67
		Students' vision and hearing health problems	13.64
		The complicated teaching software and platform	10.61
		Lack of rich extracurricular activities	7.58
		Lack of network learning equipment	7.58
		Teachers couldn't pay full attention to all students	7.58
		The unclear learning task	7.58
Enterprises	Organizations' Level	The problem of providing resource support for a wide range of suspension	100.00
	Teachers' Level	Provide online teaching support services for front-line teachers	90.00
	Students' Level	The problem of providing online learning support services for students	80.00
	Families' Level	Provide online learning resources and support services for families and parents	65.50

faced mainly concerned the adjustment of teaching work, that is, how to use the existing resources to organize teachers and students to carry out effective online education activities. To screen suitable learning platforms and resources for teachers and students, the schools taken advantage of the pandemic situation as an educational opportunity to diversify the content and forms of online education courses, and adjusted and enrich the content of courses on the basis of culture courses. At the same time, the schools organized and encouraged teachers and students to provide services for the public, striving to be the transmitter of official information, the propagandist of pandemic prevention knowledge and the maintainer of social requirement. Schools should also pay close attention to and correctly grasp the current situation of the pandemic situation, and adjust the work of the suspension of classes according to the real-time form.

At the teachers' level: As the implementation subject of online education in schools, the teachers were supposed to give full play to their own disciplinary advantages and actively cooperate with the arrangement of schools and other teachers of different disciplines to build online courses with various forms and rich content, for example, life education courses, home-based labor education courses, home-based sports health courses, parent-child mental health courses, paper-cutting courses, characteristic music courses, and so on. On account of providing these better, more interesting, and more meaningful online courses, the teachers could not only meet students' diverse learning needs and relieve the pressure and anxiety of parents and students at home but also make beneficial explorations and attempts to carry out Internet and online education in this large-scale wave of online education. Schools should emphasize that teachers ought to pay attention to online learning, not only the presentation of learning content, but also the design of the learning process. Moreover, teachers were encouraged to update their teaching concepts, realize students' learning initiatives, and create a subjective interaction mode between themselves and students in online learning.

While dynamically mastering the effect of teachers' online teaching and making improvements and adjustments within the scope of the prevailing conditions, schools also organized online training activities for experts, both inside and outside the classes, called on teachers to spontaneously form a teaching community of online education, cooperated in teaching and research, and cooperated in lesson preparation or other forms. Schools focused on training teachers and improving their online education and information-based teaching abilities, to provide greater possibilities for teachers' professional development on the Internet. During this period, some teachers with the tag of "Pop star" and "Internet celebrity" emerged, which also showed that when school education conformed to the changing needs of the Internet era and became more flexible and Internet-based, there would be unlimited possibilities. Schools also focused on training teachers and improving their online education ability and information-based teaching ability by organizing on-line and outside-campus expert training activities, calling on teachers to spontaneously form a teaching community of online education, collaborative teaching and research, collaborative lesson preparation, and other forms. This would provide greater possibilities for teachers' professional development in the Internet era and also generate some "Renowned teacher" and "Web celebrity teacher" tags. At the same time, schools were also committed to providing compulsory services to fight against the pandemic and provide large-scale social online education, including providing free education resources for other schools or the public in the form of online free class or learning platforms, providing online compulsory guidance for scholastic experts and famous teachers, providing volunteer service for teachers and students, etc. In addition, schools should also regularly test the effect of teachers' online teaching, through questionnaires, online interviews, regular tests of students' knowledge, and so on.

At the students' level: In the second stage of the schools, more voluntary service at the students' level began. With the organization and guidance of the school and teachers, students gave psychological support and encouragement to the anti-pandemic personnel with diversified works, such as poems, essays, paintings, and other works with the theme of the pandemic. Simultaneously, voluntary services were provided in the form of universities' volunteer teams, such as loving family education, psychological counsel, material transportation and management, and employment guidance, which gave full play to the role of the schools as a "down-to-earth actor" in the whole education system, and even the society. Schools should still keep timely monitoring and feedback on students' health and try to reduce the impact of online learning on the direct factors of vision, such as limiting the length of online learning. Moreover, schools should continue to carry out relevant work guided by positive psychology, to help students accept the suspension of classes.

To sum up, with the promulgation of the relevant policy of "Disrupted Class, Undisrupted Learning" and the gradual development of large-scale online learning, the relevant measures gradually became clear. But at that time, no matter whether at the level of teachers, students, or organizations, schools were facing various problems that still needed to be discussed and explored. For example, during the implementation of online learning, schools also tried to explore teaching strategies suitable for relevant courses, through practice and the summing up of experience, and create a feasible and effective education program. At the same time, they would continue to do a good job in the psychological construction of online education for teachers and students and provide matched teaching support and services, so as to ensure the smooth development of the work of class suspension.

5.2.2 Families

In the exploratory period of the "Disrupted Class, Undisrupted Learning" proposal, the objective level of the families still accounted for the vast majority of the problems, but the problems of parents gradually emerged, mainly because some students' poor self-learning ability in primary and secondary schools. Online classes needed parents' participation, which increased the burden on parents. At this level, these problems were inevitable for lower grade students, which required families to overcome the difficulties as much as possible in the special period and create a good learning atmosphere for students. Meanwhile, parents were not familiar with the use of the relevant teaching platforms, or with communication and cooperation with schools and so on, which were also problems that parents encountered when accompanying students in class. This level of problem could be solved with the cooperation with schools and enterprises. For example, schools could vigorously strengthen the communication between parents, through teachers and other means, and enterprises could launch relevant online teaching manuals and tutorials to help parents, etc.

5.2.3 Enterprises

According to the existing data, with the promotion of online education throughout the country, enterprises also provided more systematic and comprehensive compulsory services, with more types of free products and longer service life. At this stage, the enterprises took the following countermeasures to solve the problems extracted from Table 5.1:

At the organizations' level: Some enterprises tried to cooperate with schools to provide more personalized services for schools, provided an evaluation system for the effect of online education effect, and provided services to help schools reduce the risks and problems of online education, so as to support the large-scale and in-depth development of online education and reduce the worries of schools. Some enterprises even cooperated with local education departments to provide standardized, unified, accurate, and systematic services for a wider range of regional online education, greatly reducing the management and implementation costs of regional and school online education.

At the teachers' level: After experiencing the first stage of teachers' exploratory of online teaching methods, only a few teachers who still stuck to their original thoughts of online teaching; compared with other teachers, they were not familiar with the operation. Enterprises still helped teachers to start as soon as possible, through the first stage of tutorials supporting the use of software resources and after-sales service.

At the student level: Students faced a large number of online resources every day at this stage, which easily to produced fatigue. Enterprises increased students' choices of ways to engage in online education and improve their learning enthusiasm by increasing the types of functions and providing more abundant curriculum resources.

At the family level: Most parents still responded to the policy of waiting for jobs at home at this stage. In terms of enterprises, they not only provided a large number of online teaching resources for teachers and students, but also provided online resources such as vocational skills for parents to learn, so as to reduce the intensification of family conflicts.

To sum up, in the second stage, enterprises paid more attention to providing more high-quality online education resources on the basis of the original. Some enterprises cooperated with schools and local education departments to reduce the implementation costs of regions and schools, and promoted the development of enterprises themselves. Enterprises, schools, and the government all played their respective roles, with their strengths, in this period.

5.3 The policy-oriented interaction of schools, enterprises, and families

In the second stage, the government began to deploy the policy of "Disrupted Class, Undisrupted Learning," and enterprises remained highly active. Compared with the previous stage, enterprises in this stage tried to cooperate with schools or local education departments to provide more systematic and comprehensive compulsory services, and the cooperation between enterprises and schools was much closer. At the same time, schools were also involved in the development of online education resources, actively taking countermeasures for home-based teaching and emphasizing home–school cooperation, for close cooperation with families was the basis for the schools in carrying out online education. Still in a relatively passive state, families cooperated with the work of schools and strengthened the supervision and discipline of their children. During this stage, the score of the positive degree of the actions taken by each subject is: Enterprises > Schools > Families, which indicates that the enterprises in the second stage had the highest positive degree of taking action under the policy guidance, followed by the schools, which belonged to the good level, and the families had the lowest positive degree, which was in the general level. The specific interaction is shown in Figure 5.1.

With the work of "Disrupted Class, Undisrupted Learning" entering the exploratory period, under the guidance of the government's policy in this activity, the interaction between schools and enterprises was the closest. Enterprises ensured the continuous implementation of online education by providing online education resources and platforms, online teaching programs, technical support and guarantees, and teacher training. For one thing, with the help of resources provided by enterprises, schools could better develop online learning education resources and carry out teacher training. For another, schools could also give enterprises better development, and both sides could benefit and develop together. In addition, the relationship between enterprises and families was also relatively close. In the case of providing resources for schools, enterprises didn't forget to provide relevant resources for families. At the same time, they should ensure that online education to carry out smoothly between families and schools. For example,

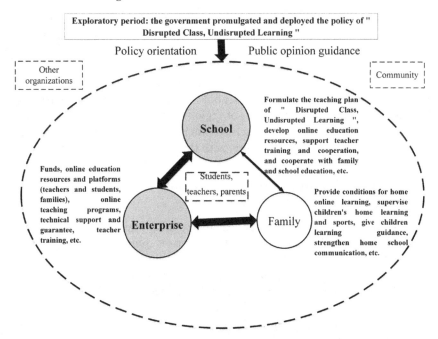

Figure 5.1 Interactive relationship chart of three main subjects under the guidance of policy in the exploratory period

under the technical support and guarantee provided by some enterprises, home–school cooperation could be realized effectively, and parents could give children learning guidance and supervision, relying on relevant information resource platforms and technology. Conversely, both the relationship between enterprises and families and the relationship between schools and families were weak.

6 The third stage

Fully deployed period

6.1 The policy orientation of government

After the "Learning Continues during Class Suspension" activity entered the fully deployed period, the government basically formed a relatively mature set of policy-oriented strategies in the first and second stages, in terms of the four dimensions of the education departments, the schools, the teachers, and the families. In the third stage, the government mainly made subtle adjustments and improvements to the policies given the feedback from schools, enterprises and families, as shown in Table C3 of Appendix C.

In the fully deployed period of the "Disrupted Class, Undisrupted Learning" activity, the government implemented the intervention mainly on local bureaus of education, schools, and enterprises, especially intensifying the instruction of the problems faced by teachers in practice, as well as the arrangement of the full opening of domestic schools, while a formulation about the families could be hardly seen. Thus, with the launching of the activity of "Classes Suspended but Learning Continues", the government adjusted the deployment of official policies according to actual situations. After the proposal and exploratory period, the government gave both overall deployment and individualized instruction to schools, enterprises, and families in the whole education ecosystem.

6.2 The policy-oriented actions of schools, families, and enterprises

With the guidance of policy in the third stage, the problems confronted by schools, families, and enterprises were as shown in Table 6.1.

To overcome the foregoing problems, the main countermeasures taken by schools, families, and enterprises are as follows:

6.2.1 Schools

At the organizations' level: After the preliminary exploration and attempt, compared to the first and second stages, the problems of the schools in the third stage were more adapted to reality. Most of these problems were left over from the first two stages and had not been solved completely, or they were new ones, extended and developed on the basis of the originals after

DOI: 10.4324/9781003188261-6

Table 6.1 The difficulties encountered by schools, families, and enterprises in the fully deployed period

Subject	Difficulties encountered		Proportion%
Schools	Organizations' Level	The support services of online learning for teachers and students	78.18
		The deployment of schools' opening work	72.73
		The provision of services for the public	69.09
		The rearrangement and adjustment of courses	63.64
		The guarantee of online learning for all students	43.64
		The overall plan and promotion of teachers' teaching progress	34.55
		The guarantee of the review work of students of junior 3 and senior 3	16.36
		The employment of graduates	9.09
		The examination of the candidates for art colleges	7.27
	Teachers' Level	The implementation of online teaching	49.09
		The provision of online learning for students	38.18
		The effect of students' online learning	20.00
		The challenge of online teaching in suspended classes	5.45
	Students' Level	The reduction of the harm to students' eyesight caused by online education	29.09
		The contribution to fight against the COVID-19 pandemic	27.27
		The timely detection and feedback of students' health	21.82
Families	Students' Level	Students' self-control	43.33
		Students' study efficiency	23.33
		Students' learning attitude	15
		The unreasonable arrangement of learning	15
		The operation of computer software	15
		Students' poor attention in learning	11.67
	Parents' Level	Whether to postpone the entrance examination of high schools and colleges or not	25
		The lack of communication with teachers	21.67
		A great deal of time with child/children	21.67
		The increase of parents' burdens	16.67
		The operation of computer software	13.33

(*Continued*)

Subject	Difficulties encountered		Proportion%
Enterprises	Objective Level	The persistent problem of network devices	31.67
		The disappointing effect of learning	28.33
		The variety of online education software	23.33
		The strenuous learning tasks	20
		The health of students' eyesight and hearing	20
		The lack of interaction between teachers and students	16.67
		The poor study atmosphere	15
		Bad learning environment	11.67
		Lack of timely supervision	11.67
		Teachers' being unfamiliar with the operation of network software	10
		The faultiness of online learning equipment	6.67
	Organizations' Level	The problem of providing resource support for a wide range of suspensions	100.00
	Teachers' Level	The problem of supplying online teaching support service for front-line teachers	94.59
	Students' Level	The provision of support services for online learning for students	97.30
	Families' Level	The provision of support services and online learning resources for families	25.00

in-depth exploration. At this time, the schools were taking positive attitudes as well as exploring a more effective and systematic way of larger-scale online education, while the solutions explored were more detailed and profound. this showed that schools at all levels had gradually found a more feasible online education scheme suitable for their own schools, based on the experience of others and the instructions of relevant experts or leading departments.

For coping with the coming work of returning to school, the schools have established a series of epidemic preventions and controls. At the same time, they continue to attach great importance to the adjustment of course content, the learning gains, and the physical and mental health of students. For instance, limiting the time of online learning to avoid the eyesight problems brought by long-time study, especially for elementary and junior students, the schools would also remind students to take vision health care seriously, and do eye exercises at rest. Some even have a unified arrangement of eye exercises, gymnastics, or other activities, after daily courses.

Simultaneously, the online courses provided by schools became more and more diversified, and their contents were connected with the students' actual lives. Except for academic subjects, there were additional courses, such as patriotism education, life education, psychological health education, labor education, family relationship education, etc. In addition, attention was paid to make a work handover of returning to school, so as to avoid possible confusion. Faced with the employment situation disrupted by the pandemic, the Ministry of Education issued a notice requiring innovation and the promotion of online employment services, encouraging online interviews and contract-signing. Meanwhile, schools were supposed to instruct students to timely adjust their graduation design scheme, to help them successfully complete their papers and projects, encourage students to take advantage of free access to a variety of academic resources during the epidemic period for perfecting their own researches, and find more paths to employment after graduation.

At the teachers' level: Schools, especially colleges and universities, attached much weight to their social value, building teams of experts and volunteer teachers to provide voluntary services for students, communities, the unfortunate, and the disabled. The teaching methods of teachers in online education were becoming more and more diverse, flexible, and pluralistic, and were no longer confined only to online live broadcasts or unified recordings, as in the first and second stages, but included the combination of online and offline, live broadcast, VOD service, recording and playback service, etc. Moreover, schools made the most of the existing education resources, combining a variety of teaching methods, so as to launch high-quality educational resources to meet the individual requirements of different students on the basis of full research, and assess students with a variety of evaluation methods, including online learning reports, offline homework, parents' feedback, students' self-reflection, etc., which would lay a good foundation for the implementation and effectiveness of online education.

In addition, it was emphasized that teachers should mobilize students' learning enthusiasm and ensure the effectiveness of online learning. Generally speaking, the final grade of online courses was composed of usual performance, quizzes, and the final exam. Yet, on the e-platform, peer evaluation could also be adopted in the assessment of partial courses, which increased learners' participation in learning, allowing learners perceptual knowledge from different perspectives. Moreover, teachers should be encouraged to meet the challenges confronting with the problems existing in online teaching.

At the students' level: For the purpose of protecting the rights of students from the impact of external factors on education, schools also focused on the students' learning and the situation of families, including the poor, students in the worst-hit regions, students who were left behind, students whose parents participated in the fight against COVID-19, and so on. Schools offered voluntary service with humanistic care and social responsibility for different kinds of students, such as providing subsidies, free flow, learning equipment, one-to-one tutoring, psychological counseling, and company, striving not to leave behind any student and to ensure that all students participated in online education. Moreover, if there were any dishonest behavior in the online final exams or essays, colleges and universities needed to seriously deal with it according to the regulations and crack down on misbehavior, to help create an excellent online learning atmosphere and promote the efficiency of online learning. Undoubtedly, students were the main participants in online learning, which showed that they should develop learning autonomy. Therefore, schools should be engaged in exploring how to improve students' autonomy, so as to correctly teach students to participate in social practices. Meanwhile, the schools should also analyze students' feedback about health problems, and accurately address students' health conditions. For graduates, some universities and enterprises managed to provide free recruitment information and consulting services, organizing interview training, and the mode of interview was turned to "online interview".

To sum up, the domestic activity of the first large-scale online learning has been in a fully deployed period, and schools further explored the corresponding measures at the teachers' and organizations' levels, so as to make the solutions more diverse, flexible, and pluralistic. Furthermore, schools themselves had an overall understanding about the implementation of online teaching schemes, while improving their work to ensure the success of online teaching in all respects.

6.2.2 Families

In the fully deployed period, based on the exploration of the first two periods, the government, schools, and enterprises took corresponding measures to confront the problems of families, which were decreasing to a large degree. In addition, parents and students also sought out practical instructions for online teaching, such as "Making a learning plan", "Supervising students through reward", "Creating a decent learning atmosphere" and so on. This manifested that, with the full implementation of the activity, the families, the audience in this activity in the education ecosystem, shifted from "Disapproval" to "Approval" and managed to accept online teaching. Concurrently, objective issues were increasing at this stage; yet along with the development of "Study at home", there would inevitably be new troubles. Therefore, it was normal to maintain a relative growth trend during this period.

6.3 Enterprises

After the accumulation of the previous two stages, enterprises have penetrated into many dimensions of schools' and social online education at the organizations' level, playing an indispensable role as providers and builders of resources and cooperators in online education at the level of teachers, students, and families. However, compared with the first two stages in the third stage, the enterprises were more like "Retreating behind the Scenes", supporting and cooperating silently, and returning more sovereignty on the "Main Battlefield" of online education to the schools.

6.4 The policy-oriented interaction of schools, enterprises, and families

In the third stage, the opening date of schools was officially set nationwide. Based on the exploration of the first two stages, the schools already had some general familiarity with the process and management of online teaching. Meanwhile, the schools extensively gathered suggestions from and disagreements between teachers, students, and parents, and continued to improve the monitoring mechanism to meet the requirements of different participants in online education, through feedback from the investigation of teaching. In addition, enterprises worked closely with schools to support schools' online-teaching scheme by optimizing their education products, enriching functionality, and improving compatibility and convenience. Meanwhile, families strengthened their communication with schools, providing feedback about children's learning situation to schools in time to help children to learn. The score of the positive degree of the actions taken by each subject is: Schools> Enterprises> Families, which indicates that schools in the third stage have the highest positive degree of taking policy-oriented actions, followed by enterprises, which belong to a good level, and families have the lowest positive degree, which is just the general one. The specific interaction is shown in Figure 6.1.

In the fully deployed period, with the policy orientation and public opinion guidance, and the help of community or other organizations, schools, enterprises, and families interacted with each other and took corresponding measures. For instance, schools improved online teaching monitoring mechanisms, supported teacher training and cooperation, etc. Enterprises provided platform services, technical support, etc. Families guided children to make learning plans and so on. The degree of schools' interactive participation is the highest, followed by that of enterprises, and that of families is the weakest.

When online learning was in the stage of comprehensive development, the interaction between schools and families was enhanced. In order to inform the situation of students' online learning, schools widely collected the opinions of students, parents, and teachers, while families provided conditions and suggestions and supervised children's home learning and movement, so as to help children make learning plans and strengthen the cooperation with schools, providing a certain guarantee for the effectiveness of students' online learning. Nevertheless, the interaction frequency among families, enterprises, schools, and enterprises was decreased. In this stage, online learning was developed in a comprehensive condition. The schools attached more significance to feedback about students' learning at home, and relatively speaking, the interaction with enterprises was decreased. But there were still some irreplaceable interactions. For instance, the assistance offered by enterprises was required in schools that were occupied with online teaching monitoring mechanisms and teacher training. While online learning was in a steady state, the interactions between families and enterprise were indistinct.

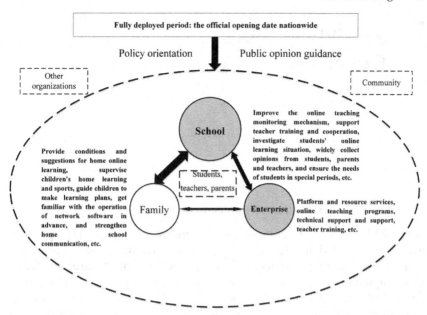

Figure 6.1 Interactive relationship chart of the three main subjects under the guidance of policy in the fully deployed period

7 The fourth stage

Exit period

7.1 The policy orientation of government

After the basic control of the epidemic, with the large-scale resumption of work and production in all walks of life, the preparation of returning to school has gradually launched, and the activity of "Disrupted Class, Undisrupted Learning" has entered the fourth stage, also referred to the "exit period" of the education emergency plan of "Large-Scale Formal Online Education". In this stage, the government mainly focused on the guidance of the schools, enterprises, and families, from large-scale formal online education to off-line classroom teaching, also called, in the past, face-to-face teaching. The countermeasures are shown in Table D3 of Appendix D.

As shown in Table D3 of Appendix D, the government started to shift the focus of overall planning to the arrangement of resuming classes and schools in the exit period of the "Disrupted Class, Undisrupted Learning" activity and provided certain arrangements and plans to the schools that were still continuing the activity. In general, the government instructed the nationwide resumption of classes and schools in the four dimensions of the education departments, schools, teachers, and families. The large-scale online education activities were gradually returning to ordinary face-to-face teaching. The government's policy orientation was essentially on the connection between protection and the resumption of classes and in-person school. Additionally, schools, enterprises, and families were taking countermeasures responding to the actual situation of the resumption of classes and in-person school.

7.2 The policy-oriented actions of schools, families, and enterprises

Under the policy guidance in the fourth stage, the main problems faced by schools, families, and enterprises were as shown in Table 7.1.

To overcome these problems, the main countermeasures taken by the schools, families, and enterprises include:

DOI: 10.4324/9781003188261-7

Table 7.1 The difficulties encountered by schools, families, and enterprises in the exit period

Subject	Difficulties Encountered		Proportion (%)
Schools	Organizations' Level	The preparation for the start of school	96.55
		The adjustment of the spring teaching plan	93.60
		The problem of how to formulate the connection plan of returning to schools and classes	90.64
		The problem of ensuring the standard-ization and order of epidemic prevention after the beginning of school	86.21
		The cooperation among teachers	75.37
		Thesis defense and employment of graduates	37.44
		Financial aid for students after returning to school	18.23
		The remedial measures to be taken when a protection vulnerability occurs	14.27
	Teachers' Level	The learning progress of students	89.16
		A scientific diagnosis of the actual effects of students' home-based study	81.77
		A scientific diagnosis of the actual effects of students' online study	57.64
		The transformation of students' learning evaluation	53.70
		The prevention and protection of students	41.38
		How to guarantee the learning progress of students with learning difficulties	29.06
	Students' Level	Psychological counseling for students	84.73
		The polarization of students' learning states after returning to schools	66.50
		The reconstruction of students' campus life	46.31
		Social services	33.01
Families	Students' Level	The problem of students' ineffective online learning	76.92
		The transitional state between off-line learning and online learning	61.54
		Problems of a poor psychological state	55.38
	Parents' Level	The quality of campus protection	69.23
		Uncertainty about the date of the resumption of classes	30.77
	Objective Level	The arrangement of teaching plans	86.15
		Health protection on campus	73.85
		The adjustment of students' learning state	66.15
		The aggravation of learning tasks	60

(*Continued*)

Table 7.1 (Continued) The difficulties encountered by schools, families, and enterprises in the exit period

Subject	Difficulties Encountered		Proportion (%)
Enterprises	Organizations' Level	The problem of how to connect the resumption of classes with online learning	77.78
	Teachers' Level	Provide suggestions for effective conversions between off-line and online teaching, for frontline teachers	57.78
	Students' Level	Provide suggestions for students to transition from off-line learning to online learning	66.67
	Families' Level	How to offer parents information about the resumption of schools	40

7.2.1 Schools

At the organizations' level: Schools made adequate preparations for the beginning of school in advance, organized the teachers and staffs to be cultivated in batches based on the division of labor, and elaborated videos of the layout of campus epidemic prevention facilities, emergency drilling, certificate of resumption of classes of students, and the "Seven-Step Hand-Washing" method for teachers and students to practice. Simultaneously, schools were obliged to take the arrangement of leaving school and getting back to school in batches into serious consideration. Furthermore, with the unified arrangement of the Education Bureau, schools energetically provided sufficient epidemic prevention materials, such as forehead temperature measuring guns, disinfectants, hand sanitizer, masks, etc. Apart from that, schools accelerated the development of a sequence of regulations for epidemic prevention, organizing all teachers to carry out epidemic prevention simulation exercises in addition to the "Sand Table Deduction". They also set up classes on "Independent Temperature Measurement", which students were required to finish at home. For preventing crowds, every class would be asked to exercise in a designated area during physical education classes. In addition, novel prevention and control techniques were required in advance. Last but not least, schools were given the task of perfecting the construction of online education and teaching platforms in primary and secondary schools, improve the monitoring mechanism for online teaching resources, and issue measures based on the reality of each school among colleges and universities. As for the upgrading of curriculum resources from "Emergency Plan" to "Qualified Course" after the beginning of school, Wu Yan argued that it is necessary to optimize online teaching service platforms and replace "low-quality courses" with "Golden courses", bringing higher education into a new era with benchmarks, role models, and standards.

At the teachers' level: Schools were supposed to pay full attention to teachers' reasonable demands, reduce or end the arrangement of various nonteaching tasks, clearly draft teachers' supplementary holiday plans, and reward teachers for overtime work. The workload of teachers and learning efficiency of students should be taken into an overall consideration while adjusting the teaching plan. Not only the actual situations and endurance of teachers in elementary and secondary schools should be emphasized, but teachers' reasonable demands should also be addressed. In this way, teachers' working enthusiasm could be improved significantly after the resumption of class. Meanwhile, teachers were obliged to give ideological guidance with patriotism education, highlight the physical and mental health of students, reform the teaching contents, and the make innovations in the pattern and method of teaching. In addition, teachers could assist students to make a smooth transition from home-based learning to schools-based learning. The formulation of teaching plans should be based on the differentiation of learning effect, prominent psychological problems, increased learning pressure, the adjustment of learning habits, the adaptation of the learning environment, and other realities experienced by students. In particular, according to the learning effects and knowledge states of students, teachers should appropriately reduce the difficulty of teaching and slow down the pace of teaching. Also, teachers ought to diagnose the learning effects and knowledge states scientifically, on account of the actual position of their students, and appropriately reduce the difficulty of tests. In short, schools, in accordance with their own resources and conditions, gradually finished the transition from online education to off-line education.

At the students' level: For the exit stage of online learning, schools not only continued to develop online learning control and guidance but also paid more attention to students' psychological situations, effectively offering students psychological counseling during the epidemic and even after the beginning of school, because of the long-term closure and isolation, which caused variations in psychological states. Moreover, the interaction between schools and families should be frequent, in case any psychological problems arise for students. Before students return, schools ought to prepare in advance and instruct students to adapt to school life as soon as possible, so as to make up for the lack of key knowledge in online learning. In addition, schools should help students to establish learning objectives and self-confidence, formulate reasonable learning plans for off-line learning according to actual situations, and encourage students to participate in the reconstruction of campus life, such as abiding by school rules and schedules. In this stage, students were supposed to be reminded to balance their study and life and adjust their learning states in time to prepare for the coming off-line learning.

In summary, in the fourth stage, schools had carried out large-scale online education for quite a long time and basically entered a stable state of online teaching. Some schools had completed more than half of their teaching tasks online. Facing the gradually stable and relatively controllable educational crisis, schools gradually withdrew from the original large-scale online teaching mode, under the guidance of government policies, and turned to face-to-face teaching in off-line classrooms. At the same time, confronted with a series of problems that might occur in the resumption of in-person education, schools have taken corresponding measures to ensure the quality of online teaching for teachers and students, and gradually prepared for the series of necessary tasks.

7.2.2 Families

In the exit period of the "Learning Continues during Class Suspension" activity, with the gradual resumption of classes, the problems faced by families began to change from the technical problems and atmosphere problems of online classes to the problems of campus protection and the connection of online learning and off-line learning after classes resumed. With the cooperation of schools and enterprises, families dealt with the practical problems in this stage through psychological counseling and the effective coordination of students' learning time.

7.2.3 Enterprises

In the fourth stage, enterprises basically withdrew from the explicit mechanism of an education emergency. In addition to the comprehensive resumption of work and production, enterprises provided support for schools, especially supporting resumption resources, including the issuance of grants, providing epidemic prevention supplies for teachers and students, and providing preferential education resources, to promote the smooth resumption of schools. Meanwhile, enterprises tried to find long-term and sustainable ways to maintain good school-enterprise cooperation for their mutual benefit and a win-win cooperation.

7.3 The policy-oriented interaction of schools, enterprises, and families

In the fourth stage, the government announced that all regions should arrange for the resumption of classes according to the severity of the local epidemic situation in succession, and schools should actively prepare for the resumption of classes, establish campus emergency prevention and control mechanisms during the pandemic, and become leaders in this education emergency. Meanwhile, enterprises continued to provide teachers and students with online and off-line education resources. Some enterprises were seeking a long-term cooperation with schools. Moreover, some institutions in low-risk areas started teaching off-line and fully resumed work and production. At the families' level, parents were required to teach their children to establish their own awareness of epidemic prevention, adjust their learning status, and adapt to the school schedule as soon as possible. In this stage, the score of the positive degree of each subject under the policy guidance is: Schools >

Enterprises > Families, which indicates that in the fourth stage, schools have the highest positive degree of taking policy-oriented actions, followed by enterprises, which belong to the good level, and families have the lowest positive degree, which is in the pass level. The specific interaction is shown in the Figure 7.1.

For online learning during the stage of withdrawal, the government issued the policy that all regions arrange "resuming classes" in succession. During this period, the interaction of the three aforementioned subjects also changed, under the guidance of policies and public opinion. The interaction between schools and enterprises increased, while that between families and enterprises held the line. However, the interaction between schools and families decreased. The interaction between the two subjects are as follows. In this period, from the perspective of schools and enterprises, schools positively prepared for the start of school, adjusted teaching plans, and did a good job in campus pandemic prevention. Simultaneously, to ensure the smooth progress of "returning to schools and classes", with the suggestion by enterprises of connecting online teaching and off-line teaching that was provided for teachers and students, schools made overall arrangements for relevant teaching issues. As the large-scale online education activity has come to an end, schools have a certain understanding of students' online learning, and families have gradually adapted to students' learning at home, so the interaction between schools and families has gradually decreased. On the other hand, the change in interaction between families and enterprises was negligible.

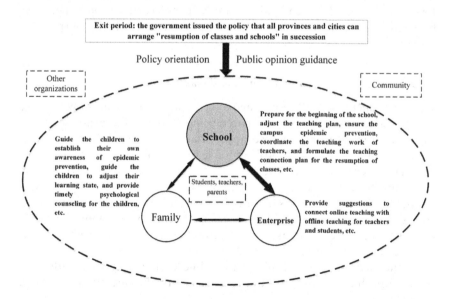

Figure 7.1 Interactive relationship chart of the three main subjects under the guidance of policy in the exit period

8 Discussion

8.1 The interaction between the four agents

8.1.1 Interaction between government and schools

In the process, the government provided guidance and suggestions to schools through the issuance of policies, and schools flexibly carried out online education in accordance with those policies. From a passive response to government policy at the beginning, to the later development of executable online education work plans, organizing experts and teachers, schools actively explored and gradually implemented online education, making large-scale formal online education possible. The measures taken by the schools were mainly to solve the core problems of the three dimensions of "How schools respond to 'Disrupted Class, Undisrupted Learning'", "How teachers respond to the challenge of 'Disrupted Class, Undisrupted Learning'", and "How to achieve family-school coeducation". This was basically consistent with the government's concerns and the purpose of policy making.

8.1.2 Interaction between government and families

The government basically combined a series of problems faced by families and gave relevant suggestions to parents and students. For example, it was suggested that students choose appropriate learning methods to learn independently, to solve the problem of learning efficiency. The communication between teachers and students should be strengthened. Also, Parents were advised to personally guide the online learning of lower-grade students, to solve the problems of their inattention and poor learning results. It was also recommended that parents strictly control how long their children use electronic products, and effectively protect their eyesight, to prevent students' vision problems. Moreover, students and parents were recommended to become familiar with online learning methods in advance, to solve problems caused by unfamiliarity with the operation of online platforms, etc.

DOI: 10.4324/9781003188261-8

8.1.3 Interaction between government and enterprises

Although the government did not make direct demands on enterprises, enterprises with a "sharp sense of smell" quickly grasped the trend of education policy, finding that they could play an indispensable role in this education emergency. On the one hand, they could contribute to online education; on the other hand, their participation also helped them to create a living space in which the company could survive the (financial) crisis. Therefore, under the guidance of government policies, enterprises quickly adjusted their own operating models to fully respond to "Disrupted Class, Undisrupted Learning" and "Online Education". In addition to quickly converting products and resources to online methods, they also donated large amounts of materials to schools and communities, and provided completely free or partly free educational resources and learning support services for the public, schools, and families. Thus, enterprises were the first to spontaneously respond to policy documents from the perspectives of social welfare and corporate development. Meanwhile, policies provided them with practical navigation and new development opportunities.

8.1.4 Interaction between schools and families

Mutual cooperation has always existed between schools and families, but this was the first time it occurred on such an extensive and scale, in such depth. The main purpose of the interaction between schools and families was to help students achieve substantial gains in large-scale and comprehensive online education. The interaction included schools providing online education suggestions and guidance for families, training parents on the basic knowledge and methods of online education, and offering necessary help for families, such as learning management, time management, health management, and emotional management when students stayed at home. At the same time, schools tried to design and offer parent-child courses, to encourage parents to interact with their children more at home and improve family emotions. In turn, parents helped schools supervise students' home-based online learning, and provided students with necessary learning assistance. Schools also provided timely feedback to teachers about students' relevant information, which provided a basis for evaluating the school's teaching and health assessments, and also gave reliable feedback on students' health and learning conditions. Therefore, schools and families cooperated and supported each other, to jointly provide guarantees for online learning at home.

8.1.5 Interaction between schools and enterprises

During the pandemic, enterprises provided support and services to schools in the form of funds, educational resources, educational products, educational programs, network technology, etc. and then schools could choose those forms according to their needs, which made the interaction between them stronger in the supply of and demand for educational resources and services. That is to say, companies, especially education companies, could provide financial support for schools to carry out online education, with more targeted online education resources and products to support education. Absolutely, most of these resources and products were free or low-cost, so that they could be developed jointly with schools. From this perspective, schools could in turn provide a larger application space for the company's products, help companies test the practicability of their products, and further promote the sustainable development of the companies. While schools could provide enterprises with "Places of practice" and "Front-line feedback and suggestions", these enterprises could also reduce the cost of schools' resource development and construction, promote the development of schools' online education, and help schools adapt to the "On-line & Off-line" teaching modes in the future. This transition and development have laid a good foundation for and strengthened school-enterprise cooperation.

8.1.6 Interaction between enterprises and families

The interaction between enterprises and families was mainly reflected in the online education products and services provided by enterprises, and families' selection and acceptance of these services. That is, enterprises provided solutions to family problems, including technical problems and personalized learning needs, etc., provided free technical support, free online learning platforms, and online teaching programs, and developed a series of parent-child courses for families, such as family relationship courses, family mental health courses, product support services and feedback tracking, providing personalized products and services for families. Although there was a minimal interaction between enterprises and families, these two subjects did have a mutual benefit interaction that cannot be ignored, which was reflected by the selection trends and preferences with families' education. These reflections would affect the designing, development, and marketing of education company's products, and then it might in turn affect family education expenditures. In future, it may be possible to further consider cooperation between enterprises and families in the context of education policies, to meet the additional educational needs of families. This is not only about children's education, but also family education or parent education, thereby promoting a more comprehensive development of family education, and also promoting the diversification of the company's education products, which is more in line with the future development trend of lifelong education and education for all.

In summary, under government policy guidance, the development trend of interaction between multiple subjects is shown in the Figure 8.1.

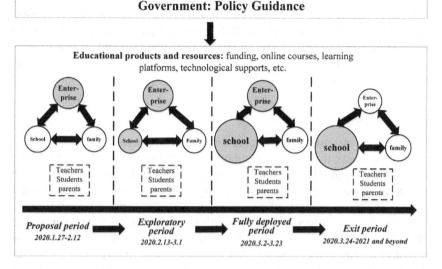

Figure 8.1 The relationship chart of the overall developmental trends and interactions among the four main subjects

8.2 The actions by the four subjects shifting across the four stages

8.2.1 The changes of policy orientation in the four stages

In the proposal period, the Ministry of Education and local education departments first made emergency plans, postponed the opening of school, planned overall for "Disrupted Class, Undisrupted Learning", and took specific measures according to local conditions. At this stage, the government mainly provided guidance on the overall direction of "Disrupted Class, Undisrupted Learning", as carried out by local education departments, schools, and families.

After the first, preparatory stage, "Disrupted Class, Undisrupted Learning" entered the exploratory period, and the government provided corresponding policy guidance for the problems faced by the other three subjects during the proposal period, namely schools, enterprises, and families. At the same time, investigation and exploration were still being carried out, in combination with the different levels of informatization in different regions.

With the development of "Disrupted Class, Undisrupted Learning", after entering the third stage, the deployment policies and guidelines at all levels for education departments, schools, teachers, and families basically improved. In the fully deployed period, the government's policy issuance slowed down; it was mainly to make more detailed and targeted guidelines based on the problems faced by the other three subjects, and to continue to supplement the relatively complete set of education policy guidelines formed earlier.

Reopen schools marked the policy of "Disrupted Class, Undisrupted Learning" began a government's past call, and the massive online education entered to the exiting period from that on. At that phrase, government policy focused on students' safety and online and off-line teaching cohesion effectively. At the same time, schools were still teaching in an online work, supplemented by related policy guidelines.

8.2.2 The changes of schools

In the proposal period, due to their relatively macro-level contents and abstract contents, the policy documents played a more regulatory and guiding role, which presented schools with many problems and challenges during the implementation process, causing them to appear relatively passive in taking actions and implementing policies. Schools, based on their own conditions of districts and resources, then took education emergency measures and arrangements, such as publishing the notice of the extension of schools, for response to government policy. According to the arrangement of relevant departments, schools canceled face-to-face teaching plans and adjusted for online education, supervised epidemic prevention and control for teachers and students, communicated with teachers and parents during the outbreak, followed up on the health of the teachers and students, and offered teaching platforms and resources. Obviously, in the first stage, schools were responding to the government's call and adjusting the work of teachers and students, keeping the same pace of massive online education as other schools. However, the effect on the promotion of large-scale online education was not obvious.

After the preparatory first stage, entering into exploratory period, i.e., the second stage, schools mainly concentrated on adjusting teaching work online, and began to focus on constructing school activities online, for example: Further screening suitable learning platforms and resources, exploring more conducive ways and forms for online education, using the outbreak as an educational opportunity at the same time, combining school resources to explore and build a variety of rich and valuable online courses, focusing on training teachers to be able to teach online, information literacy, strengthening communication, understanding, and cooperation between families and schools, and so on. In addition, schools also began to devote themselves to providing social services within their capacity, including providing free educational resources, expert guidance, and volunteer services for teachers and student teams. At this time, schools gradually took center stage on the large-scale formal online education battlefield and gradually played a role in social education.

The third stage continued to explore on the basis of the first two stages. At this time, schools at all levels and of all kinds had fully carried out online education, and schools that had not yet issued a notice of returning to school still adopted a unified way of online education to complete normal teaching activities. Schools also gradually cleared the difficulties and bottlenecks in carrying out online education. Schools began to obtain experience of online learning reforms from each other, and coordinated with other subjects, such as enterprises and families, to solve problems during the pandemic. Schools discovered more appropriate plans to carry out "Disrupted Class, Undisrupted Learning", and also established a series of arrangements for pandemic prevention and control, which paid attention to preparation for students returning to schools. And in view of problems difficult to solve, schools would continue to explore. A large number of experts and scholars in the field of online education also emerged, which showed that these problems in online learning research have attracted attention.

During the fourth stage, with the outbreak of gradually stability, although uncontrolled factors still existed, the pandemic situation in schools had been controlled. Therefore, under containment guidance, according to their regional situation, schools gradually began to determine the content of class, quitted fully online education, and returned to the previous teaching mode. The main problems for the schools were to ensure the physical and mental health of returning students, to ensure that in-person teaching was integrated with home-based online education, and to ensure that all students could keep up with the learning process, as well as that the teaching plan was completed on time. In view of this, schools in every region were to develop a series of scientific, realistic epidemic prevention programs and teaching plan adjustment programs, and so on, in order to adapt to the difficulties during the exiting period.

From the viewpoint of the time dimension of the four stages, the role of schools in large-scale online formal education trended to be more significant and critical. In order to guarantee them directly for teachers and students, schools organized, guided, and coordinated education teaching activities between teachers and students, for the schools were the bridges of connection between the government departments, enterprises, and families. Schools directly carried out the related policies and the work of executive education departments, applied all kinds of education resources and support services provided by enterprises, and monitored the quality of students' online learning and ensured their physical and mental health and safety. Therefore, we can indicate that the school subject was the core subject to effectively promote the realization of online education and the implementation of formal online education in the whole education system. Especially in the fourth stage, with online education gradually exiting, the school subject gradually restored previous education to the role of the mainland, continuing to play the central role in the education ecological system. But unlike in the past, after the education emergency, schools will play a more important role in leading the reform of education teaching methods, evaluation methods, and will also be more proactive in embrace the "Internet + Education" requirement in this era of new educational forms.

8.2.3 Changes in enterprises

Compared to schools and families under the outbreak, enterprises, especially online education enterprises and education institutions, were possibly the fastest and most active subject responding to "Disrupted Class, Undisrupted Learning". Moreover, enterprises played an indispensable role in promoting and supporting such large-scale online education. When the Ministry of Education policy of "Disrupted Class, Undisrupted Learning" was still new and hadn't even officially come out, most schools and teachers hesitated on the sidelines, while many enterprises were keen to capture the educational trend. They took positive actions, promoted work capacity, freed and opened platforms and resources, offered teaching resource bundles, provided live, recorded, and other technical support services to schools, conducted online education technology training, etc.

In the first stage, the enterprises were ahead of the schools, providing voluntary resource support and services for online education for families. Some enterprises even refunded students' off-line tuition in full and launched free or inexpensive online education resources and services. In addition, at this stage, enterprises also began to provide enterprise programs for schools to carry out online education. Meanwhile, the role and function of enterprises in the education emergency system was more critical and important than that of schools and families.

In the second stage, schools gradually entered into widespread, systematic and large-scale online education. Enterprises began to cooperate with schools harmoniously, providing students with more scientific, systematic, coherent, and diversified online courses, learning support services, and other resources. In addition to "Rooted" in schools, and got cooperation with schools, enterprises, along with local education departments, gradually provided online education methods, technology, resources, training, management, and evaluation for schools. At this time, the enterprises and the schools together became the backbone of promoting online education, cooperated with and promoted each other, and jointly sought out feasible practical solutions.

In the third stage, enterprises maintained the support and the function of the first two stages, but gradually began to play a supplementary role. That is to say, more and more students after such a long time of being educated outside of school, gradually returned to in-school education and accepted the normalized form that the priority was given to school education, and out-school education was secondary, when schools gradually played the most important role in the education system during the pandemic period. Therefore, enterprises helped more with schools that were continuing online education.

In the three stages of sustainable development, enterprises mainly provided manpower, material resources, financial resources, solid education resources, and basic support services for large-scale formal online education. The role of enterprises gradually evolved from being the initial action leader and solution provider to the "Hero behind the scenes", becoming a strong supporter of schools and the education department. For instance, special donations were made in the entrepreneur's personal name, donations in the names of the enterprises, high quality education resources were provided, management services, implementation plans, and technical support were provided for the regions, schools, and families, etc. At the same time, enterprises worked together with schools and education bureaus to provide targeted services and programs, or worked together with other enterprises to offer more optimized education services, which demonstrated the critical role of enterprises in the education emergency system, as well as their own social responsibility and national feelings.

In the fourth stage, enterprises provided a large number of material resources for schools, to ensure the physical and mental health of returning teachers and students. At the same time, enterprises cooperated with schools to provide corresponding educational resources and teaching support services, so as to ensure that the teaching achievements of online education could continue until schools returned to the previous teaching mode. Nevertheless, enterprises would gradually consider the issue of profitability, so that they could operate normally.

To sum up, through the education emergency incident, enterprises deeply realized the importance of education policy guidance and saw that the development prospect in the field of education was huge. Enterprises can give full play to the technology and resource advantage by analyzing trends in education policy, strengthening their cooperation with schools and local education departments to enhance the influence of the enterprise itself and sustainable development in the future.

8.2.4 The changes of families

The problems of families in the previous three stages were basically the same, mainly the problems existing for students themselves, the difficulties faced by parents, and the objective problems existing in online teaching, etc. We also sorted the problems of families from those of students, parents, and the objective level.

The most concentrated in the first phase of the problem was "The students' poor learning effect" in the objective aspect and "Increase the burden of the parents" in the parents' aspect, which reflected that students and parents did not welcome the change from traditional in-person education to online education in the preliminary stage of planning to carry out " Disrupted Class, Undisrupted Learning". Parents were generally concerned with the issue of "Whether the college entrance examination and high school entrance examination are postponed", which was also the most discussed issue after the launch of the "Disrupted Class, Undisrupted Learning" activity. With the continuous development of "Disrupted Class, Undisrupted Learning", after entering the second stage, the views and responses of parents and students gradually shifted from the early query to the real problems encountered in the actual course learning, which was also the most tangible feedback received by "Disrupted Class, Undisrupted Learning". The problems of families emerged endlessly. Practical operational problems began to appear in the development of online network teaching, such as "The students' poor learning effect" in the objective aspect, "Increase the burden of the parents" and "Not familiar with the teaching platform using method" in parents' aspect, "Vision and hearing health problems", "Network equipment technology inflexible problem", "Use different kinds of teaching software and platforms" in the objective aspect, and so on. Similarly, the confusion of "Whether the college entrance examination and high school entrance examination were postponed" was widely discussed in the case of poor online teaching effects.

In launching "Disrupted Class, Undisrupted Learning" for a period of time, entering the third stage, the problems faced by all levels of families basically were the same as during the second stage; but families gradually found relevant countermeasures. For example, in view of the "Learning efficiency problem" at the students' level, some countermeasures were advanced, such as "Establish learning groups to clock in and supervise each other", "Make learning plans", "Choose efficient learning methods", "Increase the sense of ritual learning", and so on. In view of the "Network software operation problems" of parents, the government issued "Countermeasures of getting familiar with and learning network teaching software in advance". In view of the objective level of "eyesight and hearing health problems", the government also advanced "Online course limited time", "Reasonable arrangement of curriculum", and other countermeasures. It can be seen that at this stage, students and parents had generally accepted the online teaching mode of "Disrupted Class, Undisrupted Learning" psychologically, and they were more likely to actively seek effective measures to deal with the problems they faced.

8.3 Summary of online teaching and learning problems in four stages

8.3.1 Changes of teachers and students in education emergency system

8.3.1.1 The changes of teachers

Teachers were passive in the first stage. With the guidance and requirements of the government and schools, teachers were arranging and designing the actual teaching of "Disrupted Class, Undisrupted Learning". When education and teaching activities were transferred online, teachers were generally faced with the professional challenges of using online teaching software, correcting homework online, recording learning resources, and so on.

In the second stage, teachers were in a state of active exploration. Based on the online teaching platforms and teaching resources screened by the schools, teachers actively adjusted their teaching methods, according to their own teaching ability. From actively participating in the relevant training of educational technology ability improvement to the independent or secondary development of teaching resources, teachers were striving to select the most suitable teaching resources and teaching methods for students in their classes. Moreover, teachers were serious, responsible, and active in interacting with students and giving feedback, fully confronting the challenges brought about by the new teaching methods and striving to complete the teaching tasks.

After a period of adaptive online teaching, although there were still many problems in online teaching, teachers seriously summarized and reflected on all kinds of problems and solutions in the process of online education, so as to explore their own online teaching methods.

In the third stage, teachers took the initiative. With the full implementation of the activity of "Disrupted Class, Undisrupted Learning", all kinds of schools at all levels across the country began to fully enter the teaching network. Teachers were getting used to this infrequent teaching method at this stage. The government, schools, and enterprises also made available a great deal of relevant policy guidance, teacher training, and so on. Therefore, teachers had basically mastered a set of relatively systematic network teaching methods for "Disrupted Class, Undisrupted Learning" and solutions to various emergencies in network courses during theoretical study and practical teaching.

In the fourth stage, teachers were basically used to the form of online education. In view of the upcoming transfer to off-line teaching, for one thing, teachers were very happy about it and looking forward to it. For another, they were also worried about the connection between online education and off-line education, the effect and progress of students' home-based learning, the teaching plan for the adjustment of working hours, and so on. However, it was undeniable that the previous three stages had achieved certain results in the training of teachers' educational technology ability, which was not only a challenge of the times but also a historical opportunity for teachers. This was different from the previous passive training of experts and the work and rest effect of seminars. Teachers' own feelings and level of improvement in their abilities should be more profound. The user habits that had been cultivated during the epidemic period enabled teachers with more skills to choose teaching methods more freely and reasonably. Therefore, the advantages of "On-line & Off-line" integrated teaching in the future would be brought into full play.

8.3.1.2 The changes of students

In the first stage, primary and secondary school students had poor self-control in learning, and it was difficult for them to concentrate on learning. In the period of "Disrupted Class, Undisrupted Learning", most students viewed online learning negatively. Of course, some students who had been in contact with online teaching for a short time had certain expectations for online teaching. In a word, students were relatively passive about, unfamiliar with, and new to "Disrupted Class, Undisrupted Learning". They carried out complete online learning activities and were also worried about the problems that may be encountered in the process of carrying out online courses, for example, whether the choice of learning environment was appropriate, whether the home network would support it, and whether it could be arranged and implemented by itself, without face-to-face communication with teachers and the help of classmates, and so on.

In the second stage, in order to adapt to small-scale "Disrupted Class, Undisrupted Learning", students found many differences between online learning and traditional classroom learning, as well as problems that were difficult to address. For example, from "Face to face" to "Screen to screen", the lack of social communication between teachers and students could be eased by forming learning communities. And long-term online learning could cause learning isolation and emotional alienation, as well as learning burden on students' physical and psychology, such as increasing learning tasks and decreasing learning efficiency. Insufficient hardware and poor network also were the problems. In addition, students' bad learning habits and attitudes also had a certain impact on learners, because they had a direct relationship with the learning effect.

In the third stage, the full implementation of "Disrupted Class, Undisrupted Learning" also meant that online teaching was the best choice during the epidemic period, for the government, schools, enterprises, and families were all cooperating and optimizing responses to the problems faced by students in the process of learning. They continued to make more detailed adjustments and offer feedback, combined with the needs of students in a relatively complete education ecosystem, in order to create a more efficient online learning environment. Students realized that online teaching would be the form that schools would adopt in the next few months. They couldn't continue to waste time and adjust their learning state after classes resumed. They gradually accepted this novel teaching method deep inside themselves. Meanwhile, they were making corresponding changes, taking certain countermeasures and adjusting their behaviors and study and life at home. Moreover, they got to be skilled at software operation, reduced the use of electronic products in addition to class time, and even communicated with teachers, who slowed down the progress of teaching, to try to resolve the difficulties.

In the fourth stage, with the continuous resumption of classes, students were gradually moving from online learning to off-line classroom learning, and gradually adjusting their mentality to return to off-line courses, on campus. Meanwhile, they were doing a good job in the finishing work of online learning and off-line learning planning. In the same way, students had to change from the state of basic adaptation to online learning to the real classroom, which was a challenge for students' psychology and learning state. For students who had already returned to school, more attention was paid to the problem of campus epidemic prevention. Students were full of expectations for returning to campus but also worried about the poor effects of their early online learning, and the prospect of the combination of online courses and off-line courses in the future. Especially after the resumption of classes, some schools would organize tests, and most students were worried about this. They thought that the knowledge from home learning was not firmly grasped and the homework hadn't been finished in time. Therefore, students had greater degree of psychological anxiety at this stage, and they were both looking forward to and worried about the resumption of classes.

8.3.2 Education emergency called for a more perfect distance online teaching system

With the development of information teaching reform and the support of various emerging technologies, education, especially distance education, had changed invisibly in the age of artificial intelligence, however, in the face of various online teaching failures, this also showed from another perspective that the current distance online teaching system in China was still not perfect as a whole, and it could only be said that relatively speaking, it had achieved some kind of success, but in the emergency situation, it was faced with the development of a large-scale online course nationwide, which was not perfect in terms of technical support, teachers, cooperation between home and school, teaching resources, and so on. Also, all kinds of education departments and schools at all levels were needed to jointly build a long-distance online teaching system for a wide range of personnel to use synchronously. Online teaching also required all kinds of education departments and schools at all levels to jointly build a long-distance online teaching system that could be used by a wide range of personnel simultaneously.

8.3.3 Education emergency to promote the reform process of education and teaching informatization

In response to the epidemic, people all over the country became familiar with online teaching and various online learning platforms and apps, teaching methods, teaching resources, teaching platforms, and so on. While these had previously been mostly the concern of educational technology specialists, they became emergency measures for the whole nation to participate in, and they were also a reflection of the first large-scale actual combat of educational informatization. Online teaching had the advantages of easy access to data, recordability, easy analysis, and good diagnosis. Since we are in the age of artificial intelligence, the analysis and diagnosis of students' data could provide personalized learning guidance and resources for students. Also, teachers could also continuously track students' learning situations based on the platform. Whether for students or teachers, online teaching was a key part of the reform of education and teaching informatization. With the further development of technology in the future and the solution of the problems encountered in the current education emergency, we believe that the reform of education and teaching could achieve more constructive results. All kinds of education departments at all levels, schools, teachers, and enterprises could cooperate with each other to explore ways to change traditional teaching and reconstruct the teaching process, in order to cultivate new talents who can think independently, and possess the critical thinking, core quality, and innovation ability to meet the needs of the twenty-first century.

9   Implications

9.1 Part 1: Summary of changes in the law of action and interaction of the three agents under the policy guidance

The pandemic has pushed online education to the frontline, reshaped the relations among teachers, students, and schools, and promoted the largest educational reform in human history. Simultaneously, on account of the lack of experience and theories, online education as the core of education emergency management is confronting unprecedented challenges. Each education emergency has the periods of initiation, adjustment, full implementation, and gentle withdrawal. As the essential emergency means, online education can't be launched without the organizational management and guarantee of education authorities, such as mobilization, emergency deployment, and process control. Taking the publication date of subtle policies as the reference for dividing the time in this research, we analyze the responses and actions of each subject under the policy situation. We can also make inferences from the discussion of public forums and public opinion, with significant response and feedback to this issue. Moreover, the analysis of the posts in public forums differs from the usual questionnaire, because of which the materials of our analysis were more representative, reflecting the real situation and public wisdom. This study combs the thorny problems encountered by all kinds of subjects in the large system of online education under the framework of the time points in this emergency cycle, discussing the corresponding countermeasures.

The schools: Formulated the emergency plan of the whole emergency cycle, carried out the emergency countermeasures step by step with emphasis, such as hierarchical and classified online education promotion arrangement, online teaching and training, workload identification, learning quality evaluation, connection with entrance examination and employment and so on.

9.2 The problems most concerned in large-scale online education

9.2.1 Infrastructure issues

The large-scale and stable development of online education is inseparable from solid conditions, especially communication facilities, teaching platform,

DOI: 10.4324/9781003188261-9

resources, and methods. For instance, how to make the network signals not only cover the whole East and West, urban and rural, mountain and island, but also operate smoothly. How can the "Internet plus Education" platform integrate other platform resources to provide high-quality and firm services? Moreover, in an emergency, there were obvious inadequacies in live teaching, blended learning, SPOCS, and other information teaching modes, and how these modes met the requirements. This raised the question, are there any suitable platforms, resources, and teaching modes for different emergency stages?

9.2.2 *The possible risks to physical and psychological health in online learning and how to avoid them*

Researchers should make it safer for children to use the Internet for educational purposes. Long-term learning online may potentially lead to major psychological and physiological issues that need social assistance and interdisciplinary research. First, online education should level the playing field for vulnerable groups, including residents with low socio-economic status, farmers, minorities, etc. However, some families don't have convenient Internet access, and some parents and students don't have sufficient information literacy, causing their online learning to lag far behind that of their counterparts. Moreover, young children need more guidance from parents, and providing this assistance could be difficult for busy parents and those with a lower educational level. Second, students could more easily obtain harmful information (e.g., pornography, violence, rumors) and become addicted to games, when staying online. Finally, children's physical health (i.e., visual health) also needs careful supervision and protection.

9.2.3 *Interactions of multiple subjects*

As the main channel of education emergency management, online education cannot be separated from the interaction among multiple subjects. Although there were many subjects involved in this management during the pandemic, the current situation generally indicated the lack of interaction and linkage among them and failed to bring a complete linkage mechanism. Consequently, future researchers ought to work on more effective multi-agent linkage mechanisms and establish sophisticated, scientific, and standardized multi-agent linkage channels and systems, from the perspective of the education ecosystem, and on the basis of pedagogy and psychology, fully take into account the basic theories of educational technology, teaching system design, and distance education, or even combine with other independent subjects, such as the community, for the sake of building a systematic and high-quality linked emergency system. School-enterprise cooperation: In the home environment, online teaching led by teachers and off-line learning guided by parents shaped a new mode of "Main and auxiliary combined" teaching. However, its collaborative process still requires discussion. Due to the differences in parents' education and economic levels, and students' capacities, online education can, as a positive learning method, easily lead to unfairness in the starting point of education. In addition, offering necessary support for vulnerable groups is inseparable from the participation of the society.

We should attach great significance to the research on the collaborative mechanism of government, industries, and universities and how to deal with the key issues that affect education equity, such as the fact that parents and students who lack information literacy can't effectively use learning resources, low-income families lack stable hardware and networks, and parents with poor educational backgrounds may not be able to give instruction to students in their off-line learning.

9.2.4 Reflection on education equity: The online education contingency plan during COVID-19 promoted the realization of education equity, in a way

Education equity is a crucial foundation of social equity, the most essential and significant equity, and the greatest tool to realize social equity. "Medium-and-Long-Term Reform and Development Policy (2010–2020)" aims to take education equity as the national basic education policy, which not only reflects the importance attached to education equity but also emphasizes the long-term and arduous task of realizing education equity. As the principal standard to measure the level of educational development, education equity is the "touchstone" to test the achievements of educational reform and development. During COVID-19, confronting the extension of schools nationwide, the activity of "Disrupted Class, Undisrupted Learning" initiated by the Ministry of Education was undoubtedly a full-scale innovation of education equity by means of information technology (Ding, 2012). Additionally, the burgeoning of e-learning could widen the channels of education, bring about the sharing of high-quality education resources, improve the quality of education, and further the objectives of educational equity.

9.2.5 Reflection on the exit mechanism

After COVID-19, online education will return to an auxiliary role in normal education. Many researchers were thinking about that how massive online education can take full advantage and be a formal action in a future education emergency. Although this pandemic will eventually pass, crises could keep emerging. Hence, based on the online education practice during the pandemic, it is worth extracting experience, consolidating theories, promoting the achievement of the goal of education informatization, and providing the experience, theories, and conditions for the next possible public health emergencies or other disasters.

An education emergency is principally composed of a prevention stage, response stage, and recovery stage. The prevention stage was committed to the prediction of a crisis, striving to take precautions against it. In the response stage, the strategy was to rebuild the education system, to restore and revise the original curriculum system and other routines. The recovery stage aimed to improve the quality of education and management. After the preparation, planning, and evaluation in the prevention and response stages, the follow-up work of an education emergency was supposed to be done in the recovery stage. Entering into the recovery stage, the workers participating in the education emergency should focus on balancing the whole education system, so as to avoid imbalanced conditions in the education emergency (Ding, 2012).

Sang (2020) argues that the COVID-19 pandemic has posed a serious warning for education, assuming that the ultimate aim of education is not to train or shape a certain type of talents, let alone to acquire simple knowledge or skills, but to focus on the cultivation of habits and abilities of students. With regard to family education, the emotions and habits of children should be taken seriously by parents, while in scholastic education, the ability for autonomous learning and peer learning ought to be paid attention to. As for community education, students' experience of social life should be emphasized. Hence, it is undoubted that if the community becomes a bridge between schools and families, it will greatly contribute to the comprehensive cultivation of students.

This study focuses on the emergency plan and process model of online education from the government (education administrative departments) and schools (school management departments), enterprises, and families.

In terms of the government, it basically played an overall role in the emergency plan of online education, mainly coordinating the problems faced by schools, teachers, and families, and issuing requirements and guidance, respectively. By figuring out the issues encountered in the various aspects of the activity, the government analyzed the problems through the relevant education departments, schools, enterprises, and families so as to solve them effectively. The government made a sane arrangement and adjustment for this activity from a strategic perspective, and along with the development in previous stages, the countermeasures of the government were adjusted accordingly. Thus, during the emergency, the government was a dominant character in overall planning and collaborative adjustment in online education.

As for the enterprises, the vital problems in the three stages of online education emergency were generally consistent, intensive, and clear, essentially concerning how to provide online teaching and learning support and assist all kinds of schools, teachers, and students during the suspension of schools, based on their own resources. As a solution to the aforementioned problems, enterprises attempted to offer adequate human resources, materials, capital, and other resources. For instance, the entrepreneur's personal donation fund, the donation fund in the name of the enterprises, the voluntary provision of technical services in partial or complete business, the cooperation with schools and the Education Bureau to apply targeted services and schemes, and joining forces for more optimized education services, and so on, all demonstrated the social responsibility and patriotism of the enterprises.

Except for entrepreneurship, social responsibility, patriotism, and national spirit, of course there would be commercial factors involved, that is, the enterprises could popularize the applications in schools and institutions through free promotion, which was of great significance in publicity and extension in the market, along with cultivating potential customers, which were also the enterprises' long-term goals for their development. Consequently, in the epidemic emergency, domestic education enterprises, especially online education enterprises, proved to be a mainstay role as the crucial battlefield for training talent.

From the perspective of the families, the core issues confronting them in the three stages of the online education emergency were basically the same, mainly focusing on the three aspects of students, parents, and objectives. Actually, most of the measures proposed by the government, schools, and enterprises were aimed at solving problems encountered by the families, on account of which the families were the direct recipients of the activity. Also, the matters they came across were also the ones that were supposed to be emphasized and settled in the whole online education emergency plan. Moreover, families were basically playing the role of discovering problems and expressing contradictions during the proposal and exploration periods. With the progressive development of online education, families were gradually shifting from passive proposers to positive problem solvers. Students and parents began to accept the teaching mode of online education, attempting to find an appropriate way to settle disputes, which indicated that the activity of "Disrupted Class, Undisrupted Learning" has achieved a certain success. Thus, in the emergency response to the COVID-19 outbreak, families, the actual experiencers in this emergency ecosystem, provided cooperation and support for the development of the activity of "Disrupted Class, Undisrupted Learning", to a certain extent.

9.3 Part 2: Reflections on the fundamental problems of online teaching in primary and secondary schools and educational innovation

With the full resumption of primary and secondary schools in the late period of "Fighting COVID-19" in 2020, online teaching across the country entered a new stage of development. However, there is still a long way to go in basic education for online teaching to change from "Freshness" to "New normal" and realize the transformation from formal "Online" to the real "In use" and "Learning" states, based on internal needs. Therefore, further research and exploration are still needed. In addition, as an educational emergency means to deal with major disasters, the education industry also needs to be well prepared to carry out large-scale and long-term online teaching, so the experience summary and reflection after the event are also indispensable. In particular, people are asking, what are the fundamental problems with the widespread use of online education in the fight against an epidemic? Where is the direction of breakthroughs and improvement? Is it possible to do better in the future?

Answers to these questions are not uncommon. Generally speaking, scholars used to think about online teaching from the perspective of what and how it should be, and less from the perspective of its subjects (teachers and students), especially from the perspective of students, what kind of presence it is as the subject of learning. Therefore, this book intends to open up another way of thinking, trying to analyze the situation from the angle of ontology. In fact, although teachers and students present two different aspects, they are by no means isolated, but a typical relational presence ("coexistence"). When we understand teachers and students from the perspective of "coexistence", and look back at online teaching from this perspective, we may discover the essence of problems and ideas for improvement in online teaching.

Furthermore, online learning (or online learning from a student's perspective) as discussed in this book refers to a formal approach to learning. Online learning has long been a form of informal learning, with formal learning still confined to schools, where institutionalized education takes place. However, "Disrupted Class, Undisrupted Learning" makes online learning a formal learning role (Huang, 2020a). Influenced by the popularity of network and online education resources, it is reasonable to believe that online teaching will continue to play a positive role in informal learning in the future, to support learners to carry out fragmented learning anytime, anywhere. Nevertheless, it is worth discussing whether online teaching will continue to play a positive role in formal learning, whether it is used as an emergency teaching method or a normal teaching method in the future.

9.3.1 Phenomenon observation: Five types of problems that affect the effectiveness of online teaching

As a major measure to be taken during an education emergency, online teaching should be recognized as having made an important contribution to the fight against the pandemic in 2020, achieving overall success. However, the rush to online education is not without criticism from teachers, students, and parents. In this regard, researchers have also produced a great deal of analysis and published a large number of articles with reflections and countermeasures. To sum up, the main problems of online teaching are as follows:

The first is the problem of teachers. The emergent large-scale online education has higher requirements for the application of technology, and some teachers are deficient in online teaching ability and information literacy, and some older teachers are more embarrassed (Huang, 2020a and b; Wang, 2020; Wu, 2020). Although some schools encourage teachers' teamwork, cooperation effect is not good reflected in the level of collective lesson preparation and lack of teamwork in teaching (Zhang, 2020a).

The second is the problem of students. Because teachers and students are in different geographical spaces, the dominant factors affecting the effect of online teaching shift from teachers to students. Students' adaptability, self-learning ability, and self-discipline are of great importance (Huang, 2020a). However, the practice shows that during the online teaching period, students' consciousness and self-discipline are generally insufficient, their independent learning ability can't meet the requirements of online teaching, and they mainly focus on shallow knowledge learning, and lack collaborative learning and deep learning (Zhang, 2020a). Through the mediating effect of family background, these deficiencies further magnify the learning gap among students, and the phenomenon of polarization is more common, resulting in an imbalance in secondary education (Huang, 2020; Zhang, 2020b). For this reason, some people argue that online teaching can create the Matthew Effect, which disadvantages children from disadvantaged families (Zhou, 2020b). There are also emotional control issues, with long hours of online learning leading to anxiety caused by physical isolation, discomfort caused by frequent cross-platform learning, and mood swings caused by changing epidemics and family conflicts (Li & Zhu, 2020).

Third is the problem of the teaching environment. The isolation of physical time and space not only makes teachers unable to control students but also leads to the obstacles of fairness and justice in examinations (Wang, 2020). Even in terms of virtual space, due to the lack of a unified integration platform, teachers often need to switch between multiple virtual spaces (teaching or communication platforms), and the "partition" between such virtual spaces can easily increase the burden on teachers and affect the fluency of teaching. The degree of fluency is often limited by network conditions. For example, a large number of teachers and students live broadcast, on-demand broadcast, and download resources at the same time, making it easy to slow down or cut off network in places with poor network conditions (Huang, 2020c; Wu, 2020). As another example, considering the network condition, with realistic factors such as the traffic burden, teachers sometimes (such as when taking attendance or asking questions) require students to "Show", while most of the time, students can be "Invisible". Such "Partial presence" makes it impossible for teachers to observe students' behaviors and reflection as in the past classroom teaching to understand their learning state. Even if students are engaged in activities unrelated to online teaching, they will not be found out, thus further increasing the sense of alienation between teachers and students and reducing the teaching effect.

Fourth is the problem of teaching resources. For now, the education resources, such as electronic teaching materials, audio-visual resources, and online courses developed by all kinds of schools and education institutions, as well as Ministry of Education projects such as "A teacher a famous lesson, a lesson a famous teacher", "Three classrooms", etc., they have accumulated a significant amount under government policy. So, there was no problem in the education resources stock, but providing high-quality education resources and difficulties also involved meeting the need for individualized teaching (Huang, 2020). The online teaching courses developed by some schools, especially taped courses, are not attractive in themselves, but students are forced to learn from them, which sometimes leads to a rebellious psychology (Huang, 2020). More important, the teaching process is dynamically generated in nature. And no matter how excellent the external educational resources as "Others" are, they can only play their role if they are integrated with the endogenous personalized teaching experience and habits of teachers, which is not an easy process to absorb and integrate (Huang, 2020).

Fifth is the problem of home-school cooperation. Home learning cannot be separated from parents' guidance. Therefore, the "Double-Center" model of "Teacher-Lecturers & Parents-Assisted" has become the mainstream teaching model during the period of "Disrupted Class, Undisrupted Learning", and parents or guardians have played a vital role as the supplementary tutors of online teaching. In this sense, family background becomes an important mediating variable that affects students' online learning effect. Some parents lack the knowledge needed to tutor children, or are busy with their own careers; some have no ability or are too busy to take care of the children's learning, so most online teaching at home has to rely on the care of parents or children's attentiveness. However, the metonymic culture highlighted by the information society gives digital natives an advantage in acquiring information that their elders do not have. As long as the Internet is available, children can quickly access the entertainment resources they are interested in and skillfully switch between lesson learning and entertainment chat, while the elders are still living in the dark (Huang, 2020aIn this context, close communication between families and schools and the improvement of parents' information literacy are not only critical, but also a real problem. Therefore, home-school collaboration in the digital age will become a major challenge for future online education (Zhou, 2020a).

On the whole, the foregoing "Phenomenological observations" are similar to the conclusions of previous studies. For example, as early as the last century, two scholars, Webster and Hackley, divided the factors affecting network learning into four dimensions: technologies, teachers, courses, and learners (Webster & Hackley, 1997). However, in the face of these problems, we still have not found an effective solution. Looking at each element in isolation may not provide effective solutions. Observing the connections between elements "Back to the thing itself" and examining the underlying problems from the perspective of relational thinking may provide more enlightening ideas. To borrow a term from phenomenology, it is to investigate the "Ways in which meaning is formed in relationships", to understand the phenomena of online teaching (Vagle, **2016**).

9.3.2 Problem attribution: Five issues affecting online teaching effect

Although the description of the abovementioned phenomenon also includes the analysis of related causes, it is only a phenomenal-level investigation and analysis. This section makes further attribution analysis based on relational thinking. From the perspective of the classification of subjects and objects, relationships can generally be divided into two categories: One is the relationship between subjects, that is, ontological intersubjectivity, externalized in the form of a communication relationship or cooperation relationship; The second is the relationship between subjects and objects, namely the relationship between subjects and objects in the sense of epistemology, which is mainly manifested in the relationship between practice, cognition, and value.

Based on relational thinking, the five problems affecting online teaching can be divided into two types: The relationship between subjects (intersubjectivity), involving the relationship between teachers, teachers and students, and the relationship between home and school; and, the relationship between subjects and objects (subject-objects relationship), including the relationship between students and space, teachers and resources. All of these can be attributed to the absence or imbalance (redundancy) of the educational elements involved in the online teaching system, which is summarized as five "Whole" contradictions.

One is the "lacking in matching" of teachers' relationship caused by whole students' online teaching, namely the lack of a collaborative relationship among faculties. Because all teachers, regardless of age, gender, interest, or discipline, need to be involved in online teaching, the contradiction between whole students' online teaching and the lack of teachers' online teaching ability is not only behind the problem of the digital gap between different groups of teachers but also an all-in-one approach to online teaching, which makes teachers prepare and teach independently or divide their responsibilities based on periods or units. As a result, collaboration is weakened, and there is a lack of mutual cooperation and complementary advantages.

Second, whole-time online learning leads to a lack in warmth of the teacher–student relationship, namely the lack of emotional connection and embodied relationship between teachers and students. The physical and temporal isolation between teachers and students is not only visual and temporal isolation. Moreover, due to the psychological isolation brought about by online learning throughout the whole time period, there is only a relationship between teaching and learning. The emotional connection is weakened, and there is a lack of an embodied relationship. The teacher-student relationship becomes a single relationship between teaching and learning, which leads to a "cold" interaction between teaching and learning and the loss of "warmth" in education and teaching.

Third, participation in the whole process of tutoring leads to "lacking in responsibility" in the relationship between home and schools, that is the unbalance in tutorship between teachers and parents. Because primary and middle school students are born deficient in autonomous learning ability and the ability to sustain attention, parental tutoring often needs to cover before, during, and after class, which leads to a close relationship between parental tutoring and the work of teachers. Parents bear too much work in counseling and support, and the parent-child relationship is alienated into the teacher-student relationship, which leads to a contradiction in the whole process of participation in counseling and a lack in parental energy and ability. Among them, behind the lack of energy in parents' guidance, there is the "Working-learning contradiction" between parents' work involvement and their children's learning. And behind the lack of parents' ability to provide guidance, there is also a contradiction between the schools and parents' educational rights and responsibilities.

Fourth is that the whole home study environment causes the space relation to increase its "lacking in distance", which means the blending of the learning function and non-learning function in a family environment. Because home-based students not only occupy the physical space of the family independently, but also occupy the online virtual space, these are concentrated and unified within the family environment, granting the family space the function of whole space. Not only off-line learning, living, entertainment, and other spaces highly overlap, but online virtual space can also switch smoothly between learning, entertainment, and making friends. More important, these spaces and their spatial functions are almost seamlessly integrated, leading to the non-learning space functions becoming an important incentive to distract students' attention from learning. If students' self-control and autonomous learning ability are insufficient, it is very easy to push autonomous learning into a corner and reduce the learning effect. Therefore, from the perspective of the characteristics of the learning space, the problem can be summarized as the contradiction of "Mixing and segregation" caused by the whole home learning environment. The integration of family functional areas leads to a close relationship between learning function and non-learning function in the learning space, which eliminates the threshold between learning and non-learning, blurs the primary and secondary relationship, and the dominant and cooperative relationship between the learning function and the non-learning function, and leads to the free switching of learning behavior between various functional areas and the emergence of learning disorders.

Fifth, the demand of whole digital teaching resources leads to the "lacking balance" of the relationship between the supply and demand of resources, that is, an imbalance in quality teaching resources between the supply side and demand side. Due to the lack of abundant and systematic accumulation of high-quality digital education resources, the contradiction between the demand and supply of whole digital teaching resources arises, which is behind the long-term derailment of online and off-line teaching.

For narrowing the digital divide among teachers, it is an eternal theme to carry out the training of the teaching ability of all teachers in information technology continuously. In addition, the construction of a discipline team with a division of labor and cooperation and complementary advantages is also very important. The "Egalitarian practice of" teachers' relationship, in which all teachers are "Anchors" ("Lecturers", "Bishops"), does not conform to the characteristics of online education suitable for the co-construction or sharing of high-quality educational resources. In this sense, it is a feasible strategy to change from individual combat to team combat, allowing each teacher to have different positions in lesson preparation, lecturing, interaction, guidance, and evaluation. As part of the team collaboration, some teachers would serve as "Teaching assistants" and be deeply involved in the online counseling. Another way is to carry out technological innovation, by developing intelligent tutor or virtual tracing systems, mining online teaching platform for automatic evaluation, and smart Q&A systems. Some families can also configure educational robots, in order to reduce parents' burden to tutor their children. The balance of the supply and demand of digital resources would not happen overnight; it generally needs continuous effort and accumulation. An appropriate market mechanism is needed to lead the construction of educational resources and build up an extensive digital education resource "aircraft carrier", and realize the online/off-line, internal/external resource integration at school. After all, the high-quality education resource platform led by the state is more suitable for solving the problem of a "full stomach", but cannot effectively solve the problem of "eat well".

9.3.3 *Essence exploration: The core dimension affecting the effect of online teaching*

According to the foregoing phenomenon observation and problem attribution, it can be seen that there was no essential difference in the basic elements of teaching and learning between online teaching and off-line teaching, but the teaching environment and the structure of teaching relationship have changed a lot. As mentioned earlier, teachers and students exist as a relationship in the field of education. The impact of this important change on teaching was not at the cognitive level, but in the sense of the social existence of teachers and students, which affected students' cognitive development as an intermediary variable. From this perspective, the first, the third, and the fifth of the problems discussed mainly involve the lack and complement of teachers' sense of existence in online teaching, while the second and the fourth problems involve the reshaping of students' sense of social existence, which was also a more significant problem.

Social presence is also called social existence and social presentation (Dai & Liu, 2015). The proposal for a social presence can be traced back to the definition of social psychologists Short, Williams, and Christie: The degree to which an individual is regarded as "a real person" in the process of communication and interaction, with the help of the media (Short, Williams,

& Christie, 1976). The research on social presence in the field of education began at the end of last century. For example, Garrison and others believed that the sense of social presence was the ability of learners to truly reflect their own social and emotional characteristics through communication among learners (Garrison, Anderson, & Archer, 1999). As another example, based on the perspective of social identity, Rogers and Lea (2005) define the sense of social presence as a sense of belonging or immersion that learners obtain and realize by forming a shared social identity as members of the learning community. The definition of Dahlstrom-Hakki and others is more concise, where social presence is viewed as the interaction of a person in online learning, group cooperation, and a real-time classroom (Dahlstrom-Hakki, Alstad, & Banerjee, 2020). Chinese scholars such as Cao argued that the sense of social existence is the sum of social emotional experience generated by the interaction between learners and teaching content, such as social support and company, sense of belonging, immersion, and so on (Cao, Fu, Wang, Zhou, & Huang, 2017). Although domestic and foreign researchers have not reached a consensus on the definition of social presence, a large number of empirical studies show that there is a significant positive correlation between learners' online learning performance and their sense of social presence: Improving students' sense of social presence will help to enhance their enthusiasm and participation in learning, increase the communication and interaction between learners (Leh, 2001; Tu & McIsaac, 2002), and stimulate and maintain high-quality learning. Online cooperation can enhance learners' learning satisfaction and learning depth (Gunawardena & McIsaac, 2004; Lomicka & Lord, 2007), thus improving learning performance. However, the general sense of social existence is not conducive to practical application. What we need to ask is what aspects or dimensions does the sense of social existence embody? The answers provided by existing studies are also very diverse.

For example, from the perspective of psychological perception, Biocca and others insist that the sense of social existence includes five dimensions, that is, the sense of co-existence, the sense of participation and attention, the sense of information understanding, the sense of emotional understanding, and the sense of emotional dependence (Biocca, Harms, & Burgoon, 2003). Based on the work of Biocca and others, Kim designed a sense of social existence structure with four dimensions: Common concern and support, emotional connection, community consciousness, and open communication, and considered "Common concern and support" as its core element, because it highlights the characteristics of mutual respect and active participation among members (Kim, 2010). Zhan also revised the framework of Biocca, transforming it into five dimensions: The sense of coexistence, the sense of participation and attention, the sense of information understanding, the sense of emotional understanding and the sense of emotional dependence (Zhan and Mei, 2013). Thus, is there anything in common behind the different views? Exploring the source of a theory is an important way to enhance understanding. When we go back to existentialist philosophy, we think that no matter what dimensions the sense of social existence contains, its origin can be traced back to the theory of "co-existence", that is, the sense of social existence is the concrete expression of "co-existence" between individuals and others. The so-called "co-existence" is intersubjectivity, which is not an absolute negation of subjectivity, but a sublation of subjectivity (Zhu, 1992). Since the beginning of Descartes's "I think, therefore I am", modern Western philosophy has not only affirmed the independence and subjectivity of consciousness but also triggered the transformation from collectivism to individualism. Finally, subjectivity philosophy regards the subject as an atomic isolated individual. Intersubjectivity has the meaning of philosophical ontology started by Heidegger. Intersubjectivity involves the relationship between the self and others, the individual and society. It does not regard the self as an atomic individual, but as "being together" with other subjects, and the main way to realize it is communication and dialogue between subjects (Wang & Zou, 2008). The concept of intersubjectivity has led to a major shift in the epistemology of social science: The original "subject and object" relationship has gradually shifted to the relationship between subjects. Then the object world of human cognition, especially the spiritual phenomenon, is no longer regarded as objects, but as subjects, so as to confirm the symbiosis, equality, and mutual inclusiveness between subjects (Gu, 2011). As far as the field of education is concerned, although there are differences in teaching objectives, contents, media, methods, and modes in different periods and times, teaching can never depart from the communication and dialogue between teachers and students. Both Confucius' heuristic teaching and Socrates' midwifery are characterized by sincere and emotional deep communication between teachers and students. In this process, teachers and students are no longer engaged in a one-way transfer of knowledge or arbitrary control of power, but are communicating with each other and blending emotions into a "common" whole, which is the dwelling of virtue (emotional and ethical) (Zhang & Zhang, 2018).

It should be noted that the ontological sense of "Being together" or "Being alone" (That is to say, it is not the real "co-existence") does not mean the physical sense of distance. It does not mean that two people are "Being together" when they are close to each other, or that one person is alone when he is not close to others. On the contrary, two people who are far away in physical distance may not be distant, and two people who are very close in terms of physical distance may not be close (Heidegger, Martin, 2011). This point is particularly crucial for online teaching, which theoretically shows that online teaching also has the possibility and rationality of "co-existence". There are two forms of "Being alone". One is negative, such as complimenting each other, opposing each other, and not caring about each other. Such behaviors as following others' advice, seeking no understanding, and doing the opposite of what someone wants result from such indifference. The other is a positive style, for example, taking away other people's worries, taking over others' responsibilities, and doing things with care and love. This seems to be very positive and warm, but it is likely to make people become dependent and controlled, and even this kind of control will evolve into a kind of collective unconsciousness (i.e., everyone inclines to be similar, without personality).

On the contrary, through communication and dialogue, we can help others understand their own concerns and make use of that independently. Although we can help them, the goal is to return the concern to others eventually. In other words, the starting point of "Being together" with others is to make others become real individuals, with the ability for self-concern and autonomy. The non-real state and the real state of "co-existence" are also called the duality of "co-existence". Of course, there may be a mixture of authenticity and non-authenticity in real life (Ma, 2018).

At this point, we find that the "command and obey" mode of traditional online teaching is different from that of traditional off-line teaching. As a traditional teaching center, teachers always fall into a kind of contradiction when facing the complete online teaching environment: They can't directly carry out comprehensive interventions with students, nor can they take a laissez-faire attitude. More often, teachers have to sell "Knowledge worship" and a "Test baton", so that the teaching process points to the possession of knowledge. However, this kind of "Knowledge marketing" style makes it easy to students to lose the intrinsic motivation to explore and discover knowledge, and makes the learning process evolve into a kind of utilitarian "purchase" and "consumption" behavior, which deviates from the occurrence and development process of scientific knowledge and the meaning giving process of life growth. In this way, teaching can't become the dwelling of virtue; rather, it becomes monotonous and tedious, and the "co-existence" of teachers and students becomes a non-real state (Zhang & Zhang, 2018). In other words, the relationship between teachers and students presented by much online teaching is essentially a kind of "independent" (not really "Being together") relationship, and teachers and students lack a sense of social existence. Thus, online teaching shows familiar symptoms: Strong and mature, lonely and painful.

Needless to say, the physical isolation between teachers and students makes it impossible for teachers and students to communicate and talk naturally, as they do in the traditional classroom. Therefore, teachers and students must interact freely in some way to realize the "co-existing" online teaching process. From the perspective of specific methods, a large number of studies have shown that synchronous discussion and communication (Dahlstrom-Hakki et al., 2020; Tu & McIsaac, 2002), online feedback provided by teachers for learners, and feedback between students (such as peer review) (Cadima, Ferreira, & Monguet, et al., 2010; Sheng et al., 2019) all contribute to improving students' sense of social existence, so as to achieve the true state of "co-existence". Of course, the separation of time and space limits the time and type of teachers' feedback to students. For instance, spontaneous nonverbal behavior feedback, including eye contact and action communication, is difficult to produce in online teaching. However, online teaching also has other convenient and effective ways of communication and dialogue that off-line teaching does not have. For example, the use of expression packs and instant feedback systems is far more abundant and convenient than face-to-face observation. Moreover, at the body language feedback level, with the development and improvement of technology, such as glass-free 3D, holographic projection technology, 5G, and VR/AR technology, the shortcomings are constantly being complemented to get more feedback now. And the "sense of presence" created by visual symbol design can also be improved through careful design. In fact, only a single use of the online teaching means of communication or a single use of the off-line means of communication will highlight the disadvantages. In this sense, mixed online and off-line teaching will help to enhance students' sense of social existence.

Even so, the author still thinks that the current research's field of vision could be further expanded. From the perspective of "Being together" between teachers and students, there are six basic principles worth thinking about: Coexistence, empathy, co-construction, sharing, co-creation and symbiosis. Among them, empathy and symbiosis are the most significant. It is not only an important part of online teaching to create a sense of social existence, but also the essence of moral education.

"Coexistence" means that teachers and students identify with each other in the process of education and teaching; it is the common existence of life. Therefore, it is the basic premise to realize coexistence and the basic consciousness that teachers and students need to establish first. "Empathy" emphasizes empathy on the basis of coexistence, which is a subtle link between teachers and students. "Co-construction" emphasizes that teaching content should not only have presupposition, but also be generative, so as to reflect the value of communication and dialogue between teachers and students and stimulate students' sense of participation, achievement, and existence. "Sharing" is not only a crucial link in knowledge transfer but also an important means of knowledge evolution and group knowledge generation, "Co-creation" is the upgrading of "co-construction", which emphasizes the generation of creative knowledge and learning achievements. In addition, "symbiosis" focuses on the common spiritual growth and ability improvement between teachers and students, which is the ultimate goal of coexistence.

To sum up, the theory of "co-existence" provides an internal theoretical basis and direction for the development of online teaching. As a relatively subordinate concept, the sense of social existence can be used as a breakthrough and starting point to solve the problems of online teaching in primary and secondary schools in practice.

9.3.4 Countermeasure example: Improve the method innovation of online teaching

It is undeniable that large-scale and long-term online teaching has spawned a series of online teaching methods and modes, which could be described as endless. But on the whole, there is still a lack of imaginative and deep integration of design and practice. During an epidemic, a more important idea is to use a combination of rigid and flexible teaching arrangements, allowing students to carry out flexible online learning (Huang et al., 2020). For example, in some schools, the online teaching of each class is roughly controlled at 15–20 minutes, and the rest of the time is for autonomous learning and online tutoring, so students don't have to spend the whole class in tense teaching arrangements. As another example, some schools provide classroom recording after live teaching, and even only provide teaching videos and homework lists. Students are required to study according to a schedule, so they don't have to go to class every time, but they usually have time windows for answering questions, testing, and communicating.

In the special period of fighting against the epidemic, as a way of home-based learning, this kind of flexible teaching mode is undoubtedly reasonable. However, after the comprehensive resumption of classes, the actual conditions and needs of online teaching are reversed. Both schoolteachers and students' parents are not willing to use the online teaching mode. In fact, differing from colleges and universities, in view of the general decline of students' online learning effect, most primary and secondary schools cancel or prohibit online teaching methods after class resumption, which leads to a comprehensive "suspended" state of the various online teaching modes explored and implemented in the early stage, and "the new normal" becomes "the old normal".

Many experts believe that the blended learning mode of online and off-line integration will become the "new normal", but this needs further observation. It is certain that the flipped classroom teaching experiments carried out by some schools and teachers before the outbreak will continue to become the main implementation channel of blended learning modes. This kind of flipped classroom mainly includes two different mixed learning modes. One is the flipped learning in the classroom, which needs to rely on the smart classroom or students' own equipment (BYOD). The other is flipped learning inside and outside the school (such as: home-online learning + off-line discussion and question-answering in the school classroom). The former is restricted by the equipment available, space, time, and other conditions, and so it is hard to organize and manage, and has never been applied on a large scale. The latter mode is easy to implement, but it can't give attention to students' pursuit of high-quality educational resources and lacks the support of parents, so it has not been widely used.

In a word, the two modes have the same characteristics: First, the coverage is narrow, which is generally used as a window for teachers' personal hobbies or school teaching reform achievements. Second, the irregular and fragmented use makes it difficult to form user habits, and so it is difficult to continue. Interestingly, after the formal resumption of primary and secondary schools in 2020, online teaching showed a double trend both inside and outside of school. Because of the policy at that time, off-campus counseling institutions were not allowed to resume classes at the same time as primary and secondary schools, so they had to maintain online teaching methods for some time,

Nevertheless, there was no significant change in the number of off-campus tutorial classes, compared to before and during the pandemic, indicating that the teaching effect of online tutorial classes was recognized by parents and students. Combined with the shortcomings of the two kinds of flipped classroom, compared with the success of off-campus online training, the following three factors are very important: First, respect parents and students' pursuit of high-quality education resources. Second, make full use of spare time and get support from parents. Third, meet the needs of personalized learning.

Based on this, the author thinks that there are two other possible modes of online teaching dominated by school education that are worth trying. One is the "Trump system" type of blended learning, which can not only realize the combination of high-quality educational resources sharing and personalized learning, but also give full play to the advantages of online and off-line to enhance students' sense of social existence. The other is the online learning based "Network class system", which can meet the need for high-quality educational resources sharing, the full use of spare time, and personalized learning. The course selection system itself could effectively enhance the mutual recognition between teachers and students, so as to improve the sense of social existence of online learning. In addition, technological innovation and online platform improvement for the purpose of enhancing the sense of social existence are also necessary.

9.3.5 *The upgrading of blended learning mode: "Trump system"*

The so-called Trump system is also known as a "flexible curriculum", proposed by the American educator Lloyd Trump in the 1950s and still in use today (Xie & Zheng, 2003). The specific methods include three aspects: First, large classes, with many parallel classes together, using modern means to start classes, taught by the best teachers. Second, small class discussion, with about 20 people in each class, organized by teachers or excellent students. This method mainly exchanges and discusses the learning content of a large class. Third, individual assignments, some of which are arranged by teachers and some by students, to meet the needs of personalized development.

In terms of class hours, taking about 20 minutes as a class unit, a relatively complete teaching unit includes two class hours of a large class, one class hour of small class discussion, and two class hours of individual homework. However, the class hours and proportion of each class can be flexibly adjusted according to need, rather than adhering to a unified and unchangeable setting. It is not difficult to see that the Trump system tries to combine the advantages of class teaching, group teaching, individual teaching, and flexible teaching. Compared with the online teaching in the COVID-19 era, the practice of requiring all teachers to be responsible for the complete teaching tasks of their own classes can exercise each teacher's information-based teaching ability.

Therefore, a lesson learned from the Trump system is to take each grade as a learning unit, selecting excellent teachers or subject groups to work together by teaching live or broadcasting video for multiple classes, and then teachers are responsible for their own classes in class discussion, guidance, and supplementary teaching, according to the school timetable. The new Trump system will be a comprehensive and more operational flexible teaching mode for students to complete learning tasks independently, and it will also create an innovative application of the Trump system in this digital era.

In the process of practical application, the Trump system type of blended learning can make full use of the multimedia playback equipment in an ordinary classroom, taking the class as the unit to observe and study the synchronous high-quality teaching video, and also can allocate online course learning time to off-campus time, that is to say, the two different flipped teaching modes can be used as the specific implementation of the Trump system. It should be noted that although this mode can be used to realize the "co-existence" of teachers and students, the protection of teachers' sense of social existence and teaching rights is also very important. "The real high-light of a teacher is when he stands in the classroom, classroom is a teacher's Dojo, which is not only a sermon, but also a monastic, reflecting a teacher's greatest value and dignity" (Zheng, 2020). Any teacher with a sense of responsibility and honor will not be willing to turn his own "Responsibility field" into others' "Racecourse". Therefore, the length of shared high-quality teaching resources should be controlled. According to the actual situation of the schools, the proportions of the large class, small class discussion, and individual homework should be appropriately adjusted to leave room for each teacher to play and improve. We should develop high-quality curriculum resources in the way of division of labor and responsibility by subject groups, so that each subject teacher can participate in it and show their own value. At the same time, we should improve teaching resources iteratively through collective lesson preparation and teaching and research activities, and fully display the characteristics and advantages of each teacher.

9.3.6 Innovation of online learning mode: "Network shift system"

Trump system blended learning is mainly based on the fine-tuning of the existing school education and teaching structure. Consequently, is it possible to give full play to the advantages of online teaching across time and space, and make greater adjustments to the existing teaching structure and resource allocation, so as to realize the deep integration of online teaching and school education? The so-called "network shift system" is such a new attempt. As we all know, due to the limitations of physical time and space, there are many difficulties in the implementation of the traditional class system, and online teaching provides new possibilities. For instance, according to students' interests and differences in learning, The network shift systems selects some high-quality off-line courses, design high-quality online versions suitable for different groups of students, and let students choose courses according to their own interests and learning level. Teachers can also make the necessary selection according to course selection and teaching requirements, so as to form a new online learning class or group and use spare time for synchronous or asynchronous learning. In view of the fact that students' course selection is based on their own interests and needs, students have similar interests, which is conducive to the online interaction between students, and better course quality assurance is also easy to get the recognition of parents. From the perspective of "co-existence", the network class system can at least improve the problem of "co-existence", that is, mutual recognition and equal treatment between teachers and students. Therefore, students' sense of social existence in online learning will be significantly different from that in online teaching during the fighting COVID-19 period. This way could not only provide a new way to solve the dilemma of off-line class system but also provide a new mode for blended learning. It can fully tap into the potential of each teacher and school education, and promote the real implementation of personalized teaching, so as to accumulate and explore richer experience and a path for deepening education reform.

9.3.7 Transformation of online teaching platform: Achieve real "Classroom move"

At the level of technology development supporting online teaching, there is also room for further innovation. In a sense, the current online teaching platform, especially the live platform, is directly "transformed" from the entertainment platform or conference platform to the teaching platform, which lacks the transformation of teaching/the classroom. This is like a temporary tent built next to a collapsed classroom. Although it can provide a classroom-like space, it lacks the feeling of a classroom. After all, entertainment, work, and teaching are far removed from each other, so a necessary transformation is needed. People criticize some online teaching as "Classroom moving". On the contrary, what we lack is "Classroom moving" based on the essence of classroom teaching. Combined with the current situation of teaching platform, the main transformation direction at least has the following three aspects:

> The first is the shaping of "Sense of presence in classroom space" to ensure that teachers and students can have a "Visual presence". The so-called "Visual presence" can be expressed in different forms, such as the "Presence" of video avatars or the "Presence" of visual symbols. Each online teaching platform lacks the function of classroom customization. The concept of "Classroom" of the so-called air classroom has not been strengthened and visualized. The relationship between seatmates, classmates, and teachers and students all lack embodiment. The senses of space and distance are completely dispelled. If the students in each class can appear in the fixed "Classroom seats", it will not only create a sense of presence in an online classroom but also help teachers and students form a spatial memory, which is undoubtedly beneficial to both the teaching interaction and teacher-student relationship. And if

we can change the corresponding image tag according to the students' learning performance (such as the number and quality of interactions), for example, if the size of the head picture increases or brightens, it will also help to enhance the students' sense of existence. It is believed that with the continuous development and maturity of technology, the holographic virtual classroom based on naked eye 3D, holographic projection technology, 5G, VR/AR, and other technologies will further stimulate educators' needs for the sense of space and existence.

Second, a respect for teachers' rights is an important guarantee for teachers' sense of social existence. Teachers have the right to control the various functions of the student end, such as screen locking, barrage disable, etc., according to the teaching progress, so as to reduce the "Powerlessness" of the teacher with regard to the classroom regulation. Third, provide adaptive learning grouping and a dynamic adjustment function to improve students' sense of social existence. Whether in online or off-line teaching, cooperative learning has become a "Standard Configuration", in a sense. Traditional cooperative learning habits adopt a static grouping strategy based on homogeneous grouping or heterogeneous grouping, that is, during the whole process of cooperative learning, the members of each group remain basically unchanged. However, the learning state of learners is not invariable. The research of modern learning science shows that the group composition should consider the students' state for dynamic adjustment. Nevertheless, in the off-line or online teaching practice, whether in static grouping or dynamic grouping, it is often based on the subjective feelings of teachers and students to match the team members, which is a lack of an accurate matching mode. With the help of learning behavior analysis technology, some foreign researchers try to design different computer algorithms to explore the optimal strategy of dynamic grouping, including grouping standard, grouping method, trigger condition, and adjustment frequency, which provides the research results and development direction for dynamic grouping in online teaching. Unfortunately, there is no online teaching platform that provides a dynamic grouping function.

9.4 Part 3: Providing flexibility to resume classes in the post-epidemic period

9.4.1 Online learning makes school education sustainable during COVID-19 outbreaks

The outbreak of the deadly coronavirus made sustainability an issue in the limelight of public attention, which is a great moment to spread education sustainability. The wide and fast transmission of COVID-19 made online education formal learning in many schools under government policies. China's experience could be referred to other countries. This major disaster has blurred the boundary between formal and informal learning, remodeled the relationships between students, teachers, and schools, and could in turn stimulate a significant revolution of educational modality in human history.

While agreeing with Marco et al. (2020) that sustainable development must account for pandemic risk, we also argue that sustainability education issues should be specifically addressed under the current outbreak of COVID-19, especially for online education. The experience of China is valuable for the world, since more and more countries are facing similar problems. According to UNESCO monitoring, 85 countries have closed schools nationwide, leading over 776.7 million children and youth away from school.

On one side of the coin, since the outbreak of the deadly coronavirus, the sustainability issue is in the limelight of public attention. It is a great moment to spread the sustainability concept and think about future epidemics. What should we tell our kids about this disaster? The issue in real life is the best textbook. The whole society needs to understand a critical principle: Be kind to wild animals, and our environment need careful protection by everyone's actions (Zhan et al., 2015). From another side, government policies under the pandemic have shifted K-12 mainstream education from off-line schooling to formal online learning (Service, 2020a). Many schools have ramped up online classes to keep students on schedule. That means hundreds of millions of adolescents in China are receiving online education as the only approach to formal learning, for four to eight hours a day (Zhong & Zhan, 2020b).

To meet the new demand, many solutions have been proposed, such as online flipped classrooms, live broadcasts with interaction, teacher-oriented online teaching with off-line parent-assisted, and multi-platform blended learning, etc. More important, the traditional teaching and learning manner has tremendously changed. After the initial period, teachers and students have gradually adapted to online learning. It is reasonable to deduce that after the outbreak, when returning to campus, more teachers and students will continue to use the online approach, because the whole process has accumulated rich experience and quality resources for formal education. In addition, another important and far-reaching influence is the engagement of enterprises related to online education. This closes the gap between schools and enterprise, and shapes a new school-enterprise cooperation, which provides positive external conditions to move from informal online learning outside of school to formal online learning inside of school (Zhong & Zhan, 2020a and b). In brief, the pandemic has stimulated a significant revolution of educational modality in human history.

However, researchers should make it safer for children to use the Internet for educational purposes (Chawla, 2018). Long-term online learning may potentially lead to major psychological and physiological issues that need social assistance and interdisciplinary research. First, online education should level the playing field for vulnerable groups, including residents with low socio-economic status, farmers, minorities etc. However, some families don't have convenient Internet access, and some parents and students don't have sufficient information literacy, causing their online learning to lag far behind counterparts. Second, the students would be easier to receive some harmful information (e.g., pornographic, violence, rumors) and game addiction when keeping online. Finally, children's physical health (i.e., visual health) also needs carefully supervision and protection (Zhong & Zhan, 2020a).

9.4.2 The association between online learning time and vision

The deadly outbreak of coronavirus 2019-nCoV has made online education a formal learning setting in most schools under government policies in China. Nearly 200 million adolescent students are receiving online education as the only formal learning approach for hours per day. Thus many parents and teachers worry about the children's visual health.

Actually, the problem of teenagers' myopia prevalence or myopia progression has been widely emphasized in China for many years. The myopia rate was 53.6% in 2018 among Chinese adolescents. There meanwhile have long been numerous studies on the effects of screen time on myopia, but the results have been inconsistent, with some suggesting that screen time directly impaired vision and increased nearsightedness (Enthoven et al., 2020; Yang et al., 2020), while others claim there is no direct relationship (Lanca & Saw, 2020). The inconsistent correlation between screen time and myopia make us think twice about the paradoxes that existed in the COVID-19 situation: (a) The screen time calculation is too ambiguous, without distinguishing the time usages. For instance, the screen use for learning should be different from the screen use for entertainment and social communication, which cause addiction easily. Addiction is a kind of screen use with a high focus of attention, which is more likely to cause vision loss. (b) There is also no distinction between the time spent on a large computer screen and a small phone screen, which has a significant difference in the impact on vision. (c) The screen time was usually subjectively reported via subjective self-reporting, with insufficient statistical accuracy and a burden in collecting data. In particular, most parents are antipathetic to children's screen use, which may lead to exaggeration of time length.

Therefore, we should not make a judgment on that online education, as formal education settings would directly affect vision. Conversely, because of the following three kinds of compensation effects, perhaps online education could even "protect" children's vision to a certain degree: (a) The compensation from content dimension (e.g., learning reduced the amount of time spent on entertainment and social communications), (b) The compensation from tool dimension (e.g., bigger screens take the place of small screens because of the needs of formal learning), (c) The compensation from method dimension (e.g., online platforms can accurately calculate the actual usage time).

In this sense, three suggestions were proposed to improve the current studies: First, make full use of big data technology and accurately collect screen time through learning platforms, rather than measuring it by subjective recall. Second, strategically carry out a certain full-process online education experiments for one or two semesters, and compare the students' visual data with those who participate in traditional face-to-face education. Third, for future research on the correlation between myopia and screen time, the impact of screen use for entertainment and social communication should be addressed.

9.4.3 Flexibility to resume classes: Providing flexibility to resume classes in the post-epidemic period.

After the outbreak of COVID-19, the Ministry of Education issued the extension of schools and called on localities to use the online platform to realize "Disrupted Class, Undisrupted Learning" in order to stop the spread of the epidemic to schools. At present, the prevention and control of the epidemic in China has achieved a stage of victory. Preparations for resuming classes are being carried out in an orderly manner throughout the country. However, at the same time, the international pandemic continues to spread, and the pressure of "external prevention and importation" in China is still severe, with daily new confirmed cases not yet cleared and new asymptomatic infected people existing on a large scale. Therefore, resuming classes faces new difficulties and challenges. Recently, some cities in Heilongjiang, Yunnan, Sichuan, and other provinces had to press the "pause button" to resume classes.

In order to further understand the willingness of teachers and students to fully resume classes, we distributed an online questionnaire to parents of primary and secondary schools on April 28, 2020, and a total of 1,595 valid questionnaires were returned by April 29, 2020. The survey results showed that 73.04% of participants said they were willing to return to school as scheduled, but 16.18% still said they were unwilling or very unwilling to return to school as scheduled, and another 10.78% of parents were neutral. We learned from further interviews and analysis that there were two opposing views on whether or not to resume classes: One was eager for students to return to school as soon as possible, as this group of students may not receive effective learning support at home, such as limited internet access at home, unconscious learning, concerns about students' eyesight, lack of parental guidance, and pressure on parents to return to work; the other was concerned about resuming classes before the outbreak is fully controlled and wanted their children to continue studying at home rather than risking herd immunity by sending them to school. Wearing masks and other protective equipment all day has affected their physical and mental health. Both views were very strong, reflecting the polarization of demand for resuming classes.

Against this backdrop, we hoped to promote a "flexibility to resume classes" mechanism to reconcile the needs of two different groups and explore a new path for our education system to carry out education and teaching in emergency situations. "Flexibility to resume classes" means that each family is given the autonomy to choose whether to send their children back to school or continue to study online at home according to their own conditions and desires.

(1) "Flexibility to resume classes" can help reduce the pressure of epidemic prevention and control, continue the achievements of large-scale online education during the epidemic, and explore future educational contingency projects.

It is important to explore the "flexibility to resume classes". First of all, "flexibility to resume classes" can reduce the pressure of school epidemic prevention and control management. As some students who had the conditions for independent online learning at home would not return to school, the number of returning students would be reduced, which would help reduce the workload and difficulty in monitoring students' health status, managing their studies and life, and preparing materials for prevention and control. In particular, for areas where the number of new cases had not yet been cleared and schools with overly dense campuses, the temporary adoption of a "flexibility to resume classes" mechanism was a "temporary solution" that allowed the education system to transition smoothly from emergency online education to regular teaching.

Second, "flexibility to resume classes" helped to continue the experience gained from online education as a large-scale regular education method during the "Disrupted Class, Undisrupted Learning" phase, and preserved the output window for the educational innovations generated through online education during the epidemic. After going through numerous hardships for more than two months, online education content and infrastructure at all levels and in all types of schools had been significantly improved, and teachers' information technology teaching skills, students' information literacy, and distance learning capabilities had all improved to varying degrees. However, as the return to school approached, online education was facing a "major withdrawal", which was not conducive to consolidating the important results achieved in the early stages of online education. "Internet+ Education" was a major trend in the future development of education and should not be just a "temporary job" in an emergency situation. We advocate the "flexibility to resume classes" at this time. In fact, we hope to further summarize, continue, and integrate the valuable experience accumulated in the "Disrupted Class, Undisrupted Learning", and promote the formation of a regular development mechanism for online education, in response to the Ministry of Education's opinion on strengthening the construction of the "three classes" ("special delivery classroom", "master classroom", and "famous school network classroom").

Finally, "flexibility to resume classes" can be used as a "forerunner" to develop a useful planning system for rapid post-disaster emergency response in education systems. Major epidemics have occurred throughout human history, and while this pandemic will eventually pass, the future is still in jeopardy. The flexibility mechanism addresses not only COVID-19, but also other major public health events in the future, such as systemic educational emergency needs resulting from potential geological and weather disasters, as well as small-scale school failure caused by individual and group-specific emergencies such as serious injury, disability, and long-term hospitalization. It is the responsibility of the education authorities to ensure that every student of school age has access to education in all types of situations. As a useful first attempt, "flexibility to resume classes" can accumulate rich experience and may be transferred to important educational emergency scenarios, such as tent schools and ward schools.

(2) "Flexibility to resume classes" can be selected according to conditions in the form of a blended synchronous classroom, online classroom, regional synchronous classroom, inter-school collaborative courses, school-based synchronous recorded classes, etc.

In terms of specific practices, one possible form of "flexibility to resume classes" is the implementation of "blended synchronous classroom" in conditional schools, where a live streaming platform and related facilities are built in the classroom, allowing remote students to participate in local face-to-face classes through rich media synchronous communication technology. This model can be achieved by using existing standard live streaming platforms or by building your own recording equipment. For example, we can use a cell phone with a simple network configuration for live teaching, or high technology such as 5G+holographic projection. We encourage teachers to teach in classrooms with recording equipment for students in different physical spaces, completing face-to-face and online teaching at the same time as much as possible, without adding to the teachers' workload.

For schools without the facilities to conduct "blended synchronous classroom" live streaming, the following two types of proposals could be tried.

The first proposal is to take advantage of online education across time and space, regrouping students who study at home to form new online learning classes, and providing special online courses and tutors, which can also be called an "online class system". In order to ensure that the learning progress is basically synchronized with the school education, it is recommended that schools should form temporary online learning classes for each grade level, with teachers of the same grade level taking up the task of guidance, to concentrate the teachers' strength to carry out effective online teaching and reduce the work pressure on the original teachers in each class.

The second proposal is to continue the original class structure, without creating a new temporary online class. At the operational level, there are three different options. First, we could retain the TV classroom or online curriculum (i.e., a "regional synchronous classroom") that is provided to students during the epidemic in the region as a whole and synchronized with textbooks. These curriculum resources could form a regional curriculum resource library after resuming classes and be gradually developed into a unified high-quality open curriculum platform in the future. Second, the education authorities would coordinate the development of "inter-school collaborative courses" in the post-epidemic period. A school could be responsible for the main curriculum of a grade level. This would ensure to a greater extent that the pace of the curriculum for home-study students was consistent with that of returning students. Third, each school could independently arrange for teachers of each subject to take turns to record synchronous teaching videos in their own classrooms (i.e., "school-based synchronous recorded classes"). The video would be sent to students in time after the lesson, so that home-study students could carry out asynchronous learning, and it is also a useful review material for returning students.

Since students have to return to their original classes after resuming classes, it is critical to ensure the basic synchronization and quality and quantity of learning for both in-school and out-of-school students within the same class or grade level, regardless of which option is used. Especially for those schools using the second type of proposal, teachers need to try to understand the learning progress of home-study students, assigned the same learning tasks and homework requirements, and provide the necessary care and homework tutoring support. Teachers could also provide individualized remedial learning resources for students if they fall short.

According to the current situation of epidemic prevention and control in China, it was suggested that "flexibility to resume classes" be tried in first-tier cities (especially in areas where COVID-19 has not yet been "double-cleared"). On the one hand, many students in key schools in first-tier cities came from other districts and even other provinces and cities, so cross-regional mobility to return to school could easily increase the risk of cross-infection; on the other hand, new confirmed cases were mainly concentrated in Beijing, Shanghai, Guangzhou, Shenzhen, and other densely populated first-tier cities with huge immigration traffic. Therefore, "flexibility to resume classes" was of great importance to the prevention and control of the epidemic in first-tier cities. In addition, schools in first-tier cities were more likely to have the necessary conditions for "flexibility to resume classes". They had advantages in terms of the hardware environment, teachers' information literacy, online learning conditions for students' families, and parents' guidance ability.

It should be emphasized that "flexibility to resume classes" must adhere to the principle of voluntary choice, not be mandatory, and not trying to be one-size-fits-all. We should fully respect the wishes of parents and students.

This is mainly for non-graduating students, who have no pressure to graduate and go on to higher education and have more room for flexible resumption. In addition, "flexibility to resume classes" may increase the workload of some key teachers; therefore, it was recommended to provide policy inclination and financial compensation.

Appendix

A Appendix A. Coding process table for the government during the proposal period

Combined with the coding mode of the government in the first stage of the proposal period in a 2.4 coding scheme, this section carries out three rounds of coding: open coding, principal axis coding, and selection coding. The coding results are shown in Tables A1–A3.

Table A1 Examples of open coding and axial coding of policy

Coding Number	Original Statement	Conceptualization	Category
Ga1	If possible, schools should actively explore the "Internet +" mode to carry out distance education teaching activities and online learning courses, and the "Zhi jiang hui" education plaza will continue to open and provide high-quality online learning resources for basic education teaching.	Z1: Provide qualified online learning resources for basic education free of charge. Z2: Develop distance education teaching activities and online learning courses. Z3: Select mature teaching platforms and decent teaching resources. Z4: The teachers should adjust the curriculum soundly	ZZ1: Deploy the "Disrupted Class, Undisrupted Learning" preparation work. ZZ2: Provide technical resources for a wide range of "Disrupted Class, Undisrupted Learning" activity. ZZ3: Encourage teachers to adopt effective teaching methods. ZZ4: Improve the online teaching monitoring mechanism to ensure the quality of teaching. ZZ5: Pay attention to the problems of students' network learning burden. ZZ6: Attach importance to physical and mental health issues. ZZ7: Provide free high-quality digital resources, e-learning space and e-learning platform. ZZ8: Cultivate students' autonomous learning ability.
Ga2	In principle, the schools used their own mature digital platforms and existing online resources or constructional courses to carry out teaching work. Extensive collection of enterprises (industries) online teaching resources of job training, as supplementary teaching materials for schools' teaching. Give full play to the leading role of "Extra High Plan" constructional schools among the vocational schools, gather outstanding backbone teachers of related vocational schools and experts from enterprises to jointly develop and produce high-quality courses, and open up high-quality intercollegiate network teaching and network sharing practical training resources. Teachers of all courses should adjust the course syllabus soundly, make an effective connection with off-line teaching after the resumption of schools, arrange teaching time flexibly, and organize students to carry out theoretical teaching through network independent learning, mixed teaching, live teaching, online assessment and other methods. Teaching staff should notify every single student about the adjusted teaching arrangement through WeChat groups, QQ groups, or other ways and do an organized job of supervision and evaluation to ensure the quality of network teaching.		

Coding Number	Original Statement	Conceptualization	Category
	The online MOOCs and high-quality online course teaching resources at the provincial and university levels are utilized to actively carried out online teaching and learning activities under the support of MOOCs and experimental resource platforms, so as to ensure the teaching progress and teaching quality during the epidemic prevention and control period. Increase students' independent learning time, strengthen the online learning process and the quality of multiple assessment requirements.	Z5: Organize students to choose appropriate learning styles. Z6: Do an organized job of teaching supervision and evaluation to ensure the quality of network teaching.	ZZ9: The arrangement of online courses should be consistent with the school as far as possible. ZZ10: Monitor students' online learning. ZZ11: Make specific regulations on time limit for students of different periods. ZZ12: Count teachers' online teaching workload in performance. ZZ13: Strengthen the training and guidance of teachers' information technology teaching ability. ZZ14: Encourage teams of expert teachers to develop high-quality teaching curriculum resources. ZZ15: Relevant departments provide network technology support.
Ga3			
Ga4	With the support of MOOC platform and experimental resource platform, online teaching activities such as online teaching and online learning were actively carried out to ensure the teaching progress and teaching quality during the epidemic prevention and control period.	Z7: Make full use of high-quality online teaching resources and platforms. Z8: Actively carry out online teaching activities.	
Ga5	Increase the time for students' self-learning, and strengthen the quality requirements for the online learning process and multiple assessments.	Z9: Increase students' autonomous learning time.	
Ga6	All colleges and universities should appropriately postpone the opening time of the spring semester in 2020, and the specific opening time should be consistent with the opening time of local colleges and universities, which should be reported to the Ministry of Education for the record.	Z10: Notice of delayed opening.	

(Continued)

Table A1 (Continued) Examples of open coding and axial coding of policy

Coding Number	Original Statement	Conceptualization	Category
Ga7	The opening time of the spring semester at local colleges, primary and secondary schools, kindergartens, and other schools shall be determined by the local administrative department of education according to the unified deployment of the local Party committee and the government.	Z11: Overall planning and adjusting measures to local conditions.	
Ga8	All schools should strengthen the guidance for students' study and life during winter vacation and require them not to go out, go to parties, or hold or participate in centralized activities at home. Do a good job in the prevention and control of the epidemic situation for students who go to school or return to school by themselves in winter vacation.	Z12: Guide students to study and live at home. Z13: Do a good job of epidemic prevention and control.	
Ga9	The opening time of the spring semester of 2020 for middle, and primary schools (kindergartens) would be postponed, and the opening time of all schools will be postponed until after February 17. The specific opening time will be announced later.	Z14: Notice of delayed opening.	
Ga10	Schools with equipment and human resources should actively explore the use of the "Internet +" mode to develop distance education teaching activities and online learning courses.	Z15: Develop distance education teaching activities and online learning courses.	
Ga11	All kinds of schools at all levels are required to adopt special methods in special periods, organize students to carry out all kinds of learning activities at home, and arrange teachers to carry out corresponding online counseling or telephone counseling.	Z16: Organize students to carry out various learning activities at home.	
Ga12	Encourage primary schools and primary schools to use the "Internet +" teaching mode to develop distance education and teaching activities or to offer online learning courses. The "Zhijianghui" education square will continue to open and provide rich curriculum and teaching resources. At the same time, the "Zhijiang Hui" will provide teaching services to students in Wuhan.	Z17: Free online learning resources for basic education. Z18: Actively explore distance education teaching activities and online learning courses.	
Ga13	Encourage the majority of children to use holiday time to acquire more health knowledge, train in sports skills, cultivate exercise habits, and enhance the ability of "Healthy life for a lifetime".	Z19: Highlight the physical health of students.	

Coding Number	Original Statement	Conceptualization	Category
Ga14	Organize and carry out the network theme education activity of "Unite as one city, overcome difficulties together – College Students in action", spread scientific epidemic prevention knowledge through network essays and network works, tell touching stories of prevention and control work, and transmit positive energy to society.	Z20:Organize and carry out network theme education activities. Z21:Popularize epidemic prevention knowledge. Z22: Pay attention to students' mental health.	
Ga15	Organize experts from all disciplines to record high-quality curriculum resources in a centralized way and provide them to junior high school students and senior high school students through Internet and TV programs.	Z23: Encourage the team of expert teachers to develop high-quality teaching curriculum resources.	
Ga16	Provide students with online learning resources and online counsel, including current affairs education, health, epidemic prevention, crisis response, and etc., according to the actual situation.	Z24: Popularize epidemic prevention knowledge. Z25: Provide high-quality learning resources free of charge.	
Ga17	The teachers in charge of the classes and the teachers in charge of the department are assigned to contact and guide students when they are learning at home, learn about the relevant situation from the students every day, and do a good job in answering and guiding the students through the telephone, Internet or other means. All teaching staff would carry out their work according to the original schools' opening time and do a good job of learning guidance for students at home.	Z26: Take responsibility for daily contact and guidance of students' study at home. Z27: Offer online tutoring for students.	
Ga18	The National Open University actively took advantage of information technology and digital learning resources to serve the needs of the public for home protection and diversified learning.	Z28: Provide high-quality learning resources for free.	

(Continued)

Table A1 (Continued) Examples of open coding and axial coding of policy

Coding Number	Original Statement	Conceptualization	Category
Ga19	The National Open University immediately responded by opening multiple platforms free of charge and fully supporting the teaching work of educational institutions. The government has combined with many universities to optimize the relevant courses of education and opened them to the higher continuing education crowd with the demand for education promotion free of charge through the mooc2u platform. Primary and secondary schools, vocational colleges, education administrative departments, and training institutions across the country could apply for the use of cloud education platforms and "Cloud Learning" platforms free of charge. At the same time, more than 3,000 digital textbooks and online ideological and political courses were provided, and only one mobile phone is needed to keep learning.	Z29: Provide free network platforms for each school to use independently.	
Ga20	During the epidemic, the Chinese teaching materials synchronous learning app - Learning-Children Chinese learning APP for children and primary schools' students are provided free of charge.	Z30: Provide free network platform for independent use by all schools.	
Ga21	The National Open University has also rapidly integrated high-quality resources and launched the mobile-phone-based knowledge service of "Scientific prevention and control of epidemic situation, knowledge enriching life" to the public.	Z31: Provide high-quality learning resources free of charge. Z32: Popularize epidemic prevention knowledge.	
Ga22	The National Open Universities would provide the teachers and students of the National Open Universities and radio and Television Universities with the support they can, make full use of network information technology and online teaching methods, start schools on time, and ensure the normal teaching order of the school system.	Z33: Coordinate relevant platforms to resolve online teaching technology and service problems for teachers and students in time.	

Coding Number	Original Statement	Conceptualization	Category
Ga23	The national network cloud classroom was planned to open on February 17, in most regions. Based on the curriculum resources awarded by the Ministry Award for the project of "One teacher with one excellent course, one course of one excellent teacher", other high-quality network curriculum teaching resources were absorbed for the students to organize them from all over the country to carry out online learning. The national network cloud classroom (www.eduyun.cn) established a unified curriculum in line with the teaching schedule and provides on-demand courses based on the textbooks compiled by the Ministry and widely used in various places, covering the first grade of primary schools to the third grade of ordinary high schools with the teaching schedule.	Z32: Open the national network cloud classroom. Z33: Provide high-quality free online course teaching resources.	
Ga24	In view of the fact that some rural areas or remote and poor areas have no network or have slow network speeds, the Ministry of Education will arrange for the China Education TV station to broadcast relevant courses and resources through TV channels.	Z34: Provide special "Disrupted Classes, Undisrupted Learning" for students in special backward areas.	
Ga25	In order to enrich high-quality online learning resources, the Ministry of Education has also coordinated with the education departments in Beijing, Shanghai, Sichuan, Zhejiang, and other places, as well as primary and secondary schools affiliated with Tsinghua University and middle schools affiliated with Renmin University of China to open their online learning resources to the public free of charge during the extended period of school opening, so that the majority of primary and secondary school students can choose to study independently. At the same time, the People's Education Press has also opened the "PEP Click Read" digital teaching resource library to the public free of charge.	Z35: Provide high-quality free online course teaching resources.	
Ga26	The regions and schools with conditions should actively provide students with online learning classes with local characteristics for free. The Ministry of education also hopes that social forces can actively participate in cooperation and provide more diversified public welfare and high-quality learning resources.	Z36: Provide high-quality free online course teaching resources. Z37: Adhere to the public welfare of network courses and network teaching resources.	

(*Continued*)

Table A1 (Continued) Examples of open coding and axial coding of policy

Coding Number	Original Statement	Conceptualization	Category
Ga27	Guide students to plan the amount and time of learning, strengthen learning and psychological counseling, do a good job in vision protection, enhance physical exercise, and successfully complete learning tasks.	Z38: Make specific regulations on the time limit for students in different academic segments. Z39: Pay attention to the health of students. Z40: Pay attention to students' mental health. Z41: Pay attention to students' vision.	
Ga28	Attach great importance to work of universities and colleges during epidemic prevention and control. The headquarters and the Ministry of Education required all colleges and universities to postpone the opening time in spring. According to the requirements of "One policy for one school", the teaching organization plan is formulated.	Z42: Issue the notice of delayed opening. Z43: Grasp the overall requirements of teaching, carry out overall planning, and adjust measures to local conditions.	
Ga29	Adjust the teaching plan of spring semester appropriately: Adjust the time arrangement of theoretical teaching and practical teaching reasonably, suspend the organization of students' internship or training in other places, and coordinate the internship and training base to postpone the arrangement of students' internship and training.	Z44: Overall adjustment of teaching arrangements.	
Ga30	Make full use of online courses to carry out theoretical teaching: During the period of epidemic prevention and control, the online courses of the MOOC platform, smart vocational education, Classroom Online, Chaoxing Erya, Xueyin Online, the Smart-Tree website, and the curriculum centers of the universities under the Ministry will be provided to the students in our province for free.	Z45: Adhere to the public welfare of network courses and network teaching resources. Z46: Provide free network platform for independent use of all schools.	
Ga31	The lecturers of each course should adjust the syllabus, flexibly arrange the teaching time, and organize students to carry out theoretical knowledge learning through network autonomous learning, online and off-line hybrid teaching, live teaching, and other ways. The adjustment of the syllabus should be announced timely to the class and each student.	Z47: Using network courses to carry out teaching. Z48: Adjust the syllabus and arrange the teaching time flexibly.	

Coding Number	Original Statement	Conceptualization	Category
Ga32	Student counselors and head teachers should actively assist lecturers in the construction of WeChat groups or QQ groups. Teachers should organize students to study and complete their homework online, do a good job in live broadcasts, assessment, and guidance online, and the teaching affairs office and relevant teaching management departments should supervise online to ensure the quality and quantity of teaching. Adjust the arrangement of practical teaching activities such as experiment, practice, and training: Suspend organizing students to carry out all experiments, practice, training, or practical activities, including graduation practice and skill competition training in school, students' residences, or other places; Suspend all social practical activities of groups or individuals and do not organize or participate in various activities with intensive personnel.	Z49: Organize students to study independently on the Internet. Z50: Online and off-line hybrid teaching method. Z51: Build WeChat group or QQ group of courses. Z52: Online supervision of the academic affairs office and relevant teaching management departments. Z53: Adjust the arrangement of practical teaching activities such as experiment, practice, and training. Z54: Use information technology to carry out remote guidance and scientific organization of graduation project (thesis).	
Ga33	Scientific organization of graduation design (thesis): Scientifically and reasonably organize the graduation design (thesis) teaching of the 2020 graduates, and try not to delay the graduation time. During the delayed opening period, teachers should arrange the students' graduation design or thesis, announce task requirements, use information technology to carry out remote guidance, and require students to carry out the preliminary work of the graduation design or thesis, such as consulting the literature and preparing the opening report, according to the task requirements assigned by the teachers. Make full use of network video, audio, telephone, and other ways to carry out the work of thesis pre defense or evaluation.		

(Continued)

Table A1 (Continued) Examples of open coding and axial coding of policy

Coding Number	Original Statement	Conceptualization	Category
Ga34	Strengthen the management of teaching service: Colleges and universities should appoint counselors or head teachers and full-time teachers to be responsible for contacting students at home (or dormitory), guiding each student to reasonably arrange holidays and school follow-up teaching, doing a good job in students' learning, answering questions, and guidance, and ensuring "Continuous learning".	Z55: Schools should be responsible for daily contact and guidance of students' study at home. Z56: Offer online tutoring for students.	
Ga35	Graduate tutors should timely grasp the status of the graduate students, strengthen the contact and guidance, provide help as needed, and establish the daily report system of the situation of students leaving school to master the learning situation of students. The school should strictly implement the regulations of student status management, flexibly arrange the make-up examination and retake in the spring semester by means of remote cloud examination and a course essay, and handle the make-up and withdrawal of courses in the spring semester. Colleges and universities should pay special attention to students' mental health counseling.	Z57: Pay attention to students' mental health. Z58:Online tutoring for students.	
Ga36	Local education administrative departments carry out online teaching, autonomous learning, and online tutoring and answering by means of Internet, TV, and mobile terminals, and strive to ensure that primary and secondary schools postpone the start of school and students postpone their study.	Z59: Online tutoring for students. Z60: Develop network course teaching. Z61: Cultivate students' autonomous learning ability.	

Coding Number	Original Statement	Conceptualization	Category
	Provincial overall planning, local priority, classified implementation, ensure safety.	Z62: Grasp the overall requirements of teaching, overall planning, suit measures to local conditions.	
Ga37	Primary and secondary schools all over the country should give full play to the characteristics and advantages of the network platform, digital TV, mobile terminals, etc., and independently choose flexible and diverse forms to carry out network teaching in combination with the characteristics of regions and schools.	Z63: Build a high-quality teaching resource database for local autonomous choice.	
	Online live classroom, online on demand teaching, students' autonomous learning, TV video learning, centralized counseling and answering.	Z64: Carry out network course teaching.	
	Ordinary high school: One case for one school.		
	Compulsory education schools, schools with a better application basis for education informatization of "City level overall planning" or "County oriented" can organize teaching by grade or class by means of a public platform of national, provincial, and regional educational resources or the school's self-selection platform;	Z65: Offer free network platform for each school to use independently. Z66: Relevant departments provide network technology support. Z67: Adhere to the public welfare of network courses and network teaching resources;	
Ga38	For schools with immature hardware and software conditions, the county-level education department can arrange the high-quality teachers in the region and organize network teaching in a unified way. For remote rural areas that do not have the conditions for online learning, such as the education departments at the city and county levels, the departments should actively coordinate the local digital TV operators to set up digital TV teaching columns and organize distance learning on-demand.		

(Continued)

Table A1 (Continued) Examples of open coding and axial coding of policy

Coding Number	Original Statement	Conceptualization	Category
Ga39	Schools should do a good job in the organization and deployment of the "Disrupted Class, Undisrupted Learning" activity (local education departments and schools should organize teachers to carry out online teaching according to local conditions, clarify the teaching content, curriculum arrangement, and teaching organization form, and pay attention to the physical and mental health of teenagers in the teaching process, as well as grasping the appropriate amount of teaching content and teaching time properly. Also, schools shall not violate the relevant regulations to arrange for teachers to take superordinate teaching, or require teachers to teach during normal rest time. It is necessary to integrate high-quality education resources in combination with the local online teaching platform and the actual situation of each school, so as to ensure that all kinds of teachers at all levels can carry out education and teaching in an orderly manner. Make full use of the national network cloud classroom, national education resources or public service platforms, National Open University Digital Learning Resource Center, China education cadre network college, China Education TV channel, "People Education Click-Reading" app, People Education website, Higher Education Press Love Course, and other free platforms to guide students to learn online or listen to watch. Teachers participating in online teaching or online remote training shall be included in the teacher training hours (credits) according to the class hours determined by the assessment. Teachers undertake online teaching, online counseling, question answering, and homework correction, which are included in the workload and performance management.	Z68: Grasp the overall requirements of teaching, make overall planning, and take countermeasures suitable for local conditions. Z69: Adjust the teaching arrangement as a whole. Z70: Focus on the mental and physical health of students. Z71: Make specific regulations on the time limit of students in different periods. Z72: Build a high-quality teaching resource database for local autonomous choice. Z73: Provide free network platforms for each school to use independently. Z74: Teachers' online teaching workload should be counted as part of their performance. Z75: Strengthen the training and guidance of teachers' information technology teaching ability. Z76: Inspect and evaluate the teaching work of teachers according to the normal teaching standard.	

Coding Number	Original Statement	Conceptualization	Category
Ga40	Teachers and students in various schools can take advantage of high-quality digital resources, such as micro-classes on a platform, network courses of general high school elective courses, one teacher with one excellent course, network synchronous courses, network studios of famous teachers, digital-resource-based schools, and thematic community services to innovate teaching methods, so as to launch the "Disrupted Class, Undisrupted Learning" activity.	Z77: Provide free high-quality digital resources, online learning space, and online learning platform.	

In order to identify the relationship between the initial concept and category, determine the main and secondary categories and use the combined qualitative and quantitative method to carry out spindle coding, and calculate the percentage of each initial concept in the total sample quantity, as shown in Table A2.

Table A2 The percentage of the initial concepts in the total sample numbers

Concept Number	Concept Name	Percentage (%)	Concept Number	Concept Name	Percentage (%)
Z1	Carry out online teaching	70.97	Z25	The time limit stipulates the study time of different students	19.35
Z2	Do a good job of post-school teaching and learning at home	22.58	Z26	The arrangement of online courses is as consistent as possible with the schools	12.90
Z3	Conduct educational activities related to the epidemic	45.16	Z27	Avoid adding unnecessary burdens to students	12.90
Z4	Coordinate and adjust teaching arrangements	16.12	Z28	Pay attention to students' vision	48.39
Z5	Provide special assistance to special groups	12.90	Z29	Reasonable arrangement of students' work and schedule	29.03
Z6	Strengthen the management of all kinds of online course resources	6.45	Z30	Strengthen the psychological counseling for students	22.58
Z7	Coordinate with relevant platforms to solve the problems of online teaching technology and service for teachers and students	9.68	Z31	Pay attention to cultivate the consciousness and ability of students' independent study	41.94
Z8	Establish working groups to formulate the plans for implementation	6.45	Z32	Actively mobilize students' learning initiative and creativity	25.81
Z9	Guide parents to accept and master online learning methods in advance	9.68	Z33	Monitor students' online learning	16.13
Z10	Promote the guidance and supervision of the network learning	6.45	Z34	Build a high-quality teaching resource base for local governments to choose and use	64.51
Z11	Instruct parents to limit their children's spending on electronic products	6.45	Z35	Relevant enterprises provide network technical support	22.58
Z12	Enhance the training and guidance of teachers' information technology teaching ability	29.03	Z36	Provide free network platforms for each school to use independently	48.39
					(Continued)

Concept Number	Concept Name	Percentage (%)	Concept Number	Concept Name	Percentage (%)
Z13	Encourage teams of expert teachers to develop high-quality teaching curriculum resources	9.68	Z37	Adhere to the public welfare of online courses and online teaching resources	12.90
Z14	Strengthen the training of network teaching ability of teachers	19.35	Z38	Provide teachers with information teaching training	29.03
Z15	Improve teachers' ability to use high-quality network teaching platforms and resources to carry out teaching	16.13	Z39	Provide decent teaching resources and instructions of network broadcast platforms	16.12
Z16	Promote grassroots teaching organizations for online teaching and research activities	9.68	Z40	Guide parents to master online learning methods	16.13
Z17	Network teaching, network lesson preparation	64.52	Z41	Insist on the combination of course learning and knowledge of epidemic prevention and control	48.39
Z18	Select the teaching mode independently according to the regions and schools	25.81	Z42	Strengthen the online interaction and communication with teachers	38.71
Z19	Choose teaching programs according to students' learning needs	9.68	Z43	Choose appropriate learning methods to study independently	25.81
Z20	Teachers' online teaching workload counts toward their performance	19.35	Z44	Instruct parents to limit their children's spending on electronic products	22.58
Z21	Examine and evaluate teachers' teaching according to the past normal teaching	12.90	Z45	Accompany junior students in class	19.35
Z22	Teachers should provide immediate help and feedback to students	48.39	Z46	Parents guide their kids to manage online learning time especially in the lower grades	16.13
Z23	Strengthen the course audit and supervision of online teaching process	9.68	Z47	Parents ought to take the initiative to master online learning methods in advance	16.13
Z24	Strengthen the contact with parents	45.16			

Through the analysis of the overall data in Table A2, initial concepts that account for less than 20% are eliminated or integrated. Thus, the coding table of the government with 21 countermeasures is obtained, as shown in Table A3.

Table A3 Coding table of the proposal period of the government

Subject	Level	Countermeasure	Child Countermeasure	Proportion (%)
Schools	Organizations' level	Deploy the preparatory work of the "Disrupted Class, Undisrupted Learning" activity	Develop online course teaching	70.97
			Do a good job in the connection of teaching and home learning after the beginning of schools	22.58
			Develop educational activities related to the epidemic	45.16
			Overall adjustment of teaching arrangement	16.12
			Provide special help for special groups	12.90
			Strengthen the management of all kinds of online course resources	6.45
		Provide online learning and support services for teachers and students	Coordinate pertinent platforms to solve the problems of online teaching technology and service for teachers and students in time	9.68
			Set up a working group to work out the implementation plan	6.45
		Strengthen the cooperation between families and schools	Guide parents to accept and master online learning methods in advance	9.68
			Strengthen the guidance and supervision of e-learning	6.45
			Guide parents to limit their children's spending on electronic products	6.45
	Teacher's level	Support the training and cooperation of teachers to improve their information-based teaching level	Strengthen the training and guidance of teachers' information technology teaching ability	29.03
			Encourage the teams of expert teachers to develop high-quality teaching curriculum resources	9.68
			Strengthen the cultivation of online teaching ability of teachers	19.35
			Improve teachers' ability to use high-quality network teaching platforms and resources to carry out teaching	16.13
			Promote the basic teaching organization to develop online teaching and research activities	9.68

Subject	Level	Countermeasure	Child Countermeasure	Proportion (%)
		Encourage teachers to adopt effective teaching methods	Online teaching and online lesson preparation	64.52
			Choose the teaching modes independently according to different regions and stages	25.81
			Choose teaching plans according to students' learning needs	9.68
		Improve online teaching monitoring mechanism to ensure teaching quality	Teachers' online teaching workload should be included in performance	19.35
			Investigate and evaluate teachers' teaching work according to normal teaching	12.90
			Teachers provide help and feedback to students immediately	48.39
			Strengthen the course audit and online teaching process supervision	9.68
			Strengthen the contact with parents	45.16
		Pay attention to the burden of students' online learning	The time limit for students to study in different classes was stipulated	19.35
			The arrangement of online courses should be consistent with the school as far as possible	12.90
			Avoid adding unnecessary burden to students	12.90
	Students' level	Pay attention to students' physical and mental health	Pay attention to students' eyesight	48.39
			Reasonable arrangement of students' schedule	29.03
			Strengthen students' psychological guidance	22.58
		Cultivate students' autonomous learning ability	Pay attention to the cultivation of students' awareness and ability of autonomous learning	41.94
			Actively mobilize students' activity, initiative and creativity in learning	25.81
			Monitor the online learning of students	16.13

(Continued)

Table A3 (Continued) Coding table of the proposal period of the government

Subject	Level	Countermeasure	Child Countermeasure	Proportion (%)
Enterprises	Organizations' level	Provide technical resources support for the wide range of "Disrupted Class, Undisrupted Learning"	Build a high-quality teaching resource library for local autonomous choice	64.51
			Related enterprises provide network technology support	22.58
			Provide free network platforms for each school to use independently	48.39
	Teachers' level		Adhere to the public beneficial of network courses and network teaching resources	12.90
			Provide training related to information teaching for teachers	29.03
	Students' level		Provide high-quality learning resources and the instructions of webcast platforms	16.12
	Families' level		Guide parents to master online learning methods	16.13
Families	Advice for students	Adhere to the combination of curriculum learning and knowledge learning of epidemic prevention and control		48.39
		Strengthen the interaction with teachers online		38.71
		Choose the appropriate way of learning and study independently		25.81
	Advice for parents	Control children's use time of electronic products		22.58
		Accompany junior students in class		19.35
		Choose the length of online learning for the lower grades voluntarily		16.13
		Take the initiative to familiar with online learning methods in advance		16.13

B Appendix B. Coding process table of the exploratory period of the government

Combined with the coding mode of the government in the second stage of the exploration period in the 2.4 coding scheme, three rounds of coding are carried out open coding, principal axis coding, and selection coding. The coding results are shown in Tables B1–B3.

Table B1 Examples of open coding and axial coding of policy

Coding Number	Original Statement	Conceptualization	Category
Ga1	Based on the local online teaching platform and the actual situation of each school, teachers were organized to carry out online teaching according to local conditions. Teachers undertook online education and teaching, online tutoring and question answering, homework correction, and so on, which were included in the workload and performance management, and do a good job in improving teachers' information technology ability and opening and sharing teachers' training resources. At the same time, we should pay attention to the physical and mental health of young people and should not violate the relevant regulations to arrange teachers' advanced, out-of-limit and out-of-class online teaching.	Z1: Teachers' online workload is included in performance. Z2: Improve teachers' information technology abilities. Z3: Pay attention to students' physical and mental health.	ZZ1: Make emergency plan by various forces. ZZ2: Provide technical resources support for a wide range of "Disrupted Class, Undisrupted Learning". ZZ3: Do a good job in the preparation of "Disrupted Class, Undisrupted Learning". ZZ4: Pay attention to the burden of e-learning. ZZ5: Pay attention to the problem of students' network learning burden. ZZ6: Pay attention to physical and mental health.
Ga2	Delay the start of school, adhere to the combination of teachers' online guidance and help with students' home-based autonomous learning, reasonably arrange students' learning within a limited time, and prohibit all off-campus training institutions from carrying out any form of off-line training.	Z4: Teachers should adjust the curriculum. Z5: Organize students to choose appropriate learning methods. Z6: Off campus training was strictly prohibited.	

Coding Number	Original Statement	Conceptualization	Category
Ga3	Maintain a healthy lifestyle and do a good job in personal hygiene. Face changing emotions calmly, understand and accept negative emotions at the same time. Learn typical characters and deeds to enhance positive mental energy. Look at the epidemic prevention and control scientifically and learn the methods of emotion adjustment. Follow the arrangement of school and teachers, adapt to the home learning environment. Carry out indoor exercise activities to maintain good health. Actively communicate with parents and do housework as much as possible. As for close relatives and friends, considering COVID-19, they can only be contacted online. Control the use-time of electronic products and make it reasonable. Cultivate new interests and hobbies to enrich your life.	Z7: Suggestions for primary and secondary school students to study and live at home during the period of epidemic prevention and control. Z8: Develop distance education teaching activities and online learning courses. Z9: Increase the time for students' autonomous learning. Z10: Strictly control the use time of students' electronic products.	ZZ7: Improve teachers' own information teaching level. ZZ8: Adopt effective teaching methods. ZZ9: Cultivate students' autonomous learning ability ZZ10: Provide help and feedback to students immediately. ZZ11: Strengthen the contact with parents ZZ12: Students choose the right way to study independently ZZ13: No organization or department is allowed to carry out off-line collective training ZZ14: Grasp the overall requirements of teaching, overall planning and adjust measures to local conditions. ZZ15: Adhere to the public welfare of network courses and network teaching resources.

(Continued)

Table B1 Examples of open coding and axial coding of policy

Coding Number	Original Statement	Conceptualization	Category
Ga4	Reduce pupils' online time, protect their eyesight, establish and improve the supply mechanism and platform of high-quality educational resources, and prohibit any form of off-line training.	Z11: Focus on students' eyesight. Z12: Provide high-quality teaching resources. Z13: It is strictly forbidden to carry out any form of off-line training.	
Ga5	Actively carry out self-adjustment and do not pass negative emotions on to children. Help children improve their mood and establish a good psychological state. Help children distinguish information, not believe rumors, and not spread rumors. Make a daily schedule for the whole family to live a regular and orderly life. Give children some space to be alone, more understanding, and trust. Formulate rules for the use of electronic products to prevent children from being addicted to the Internet. Cooperate with the school to carry out home-based learning, so that classes will not be suspended. Let the children be the master of learning and improve their self-learning management ability. Strengthen life education and enhance children's awareness of self-protection. Share touching stories of fighting the epidemic and spread the positive energy of society.	Z14: Pay attention to students' mental health problems. Z15: Limit the time children spend on electronic products and protect their eyesight. Z16: Tutor children to make a home study schedule.	

Coding Number	Original Statement	Conceptualization	Category
Ga6	Make preparations for network teaching and distance teaching.	Z17: Develop online education.	
Ga7	During the extended opening period, the Ministry of Education integrated the high-quality teaching resources of the state, relevant provinces, and schools, opened the national cloud platform for primary and secondary schools, the TV cloud classroom of the China Education Station, and the online learning platforms of some provinces, and provided the electronic version of relevant teaching materials, the "PEP Click-Reading" digital teaching resource database, and other learning resources, which are free of charge.	Z18: Provide high-quality teaching resources and the instruction of live network platforms. Z19: Adhere to the public welfare of network courses and network teaching resources.	
	Parents should be reminded to avoid sending fraudulent information about delaying the start of schools and organizing online teaching.		
Ga8	In the stage of higher education, it is necessary to carry out distance education and guide students not to leave home or go back to school.	Z20: Adhere to the public welfare of network courses and network teaching resources. Z21: No off-line training in any form is allowed.	
	Instruct primary and secondary school students to do a good job in home-based learning. All schools are not allowed to organize new classes in any form, or to hold any form of off-line teaching activities and collective activities. The practice of "Online Cramming Education" is even more undesirable.		

(*Continued*)

Table B1 Examples of open coding and axial coding of policy

Coding Number	Original Statement	Conceptualization	Category
Ga9	Combined with the practice of online teaching, adhere to the thought of "Educating Five Domains Simultaneously" that means all around development of moral, intellectual, physical, aesthetics and labour education.	Z22: Cultivate students' autonomous learning ability.	
	Actively encourage students through comprehensive reading, autonomous learning, communication, and discussion.	Z23: The arrangement of online courses should be consistent with the school, as far as possible.	
	Reasonable arrangement of online teaching classroom time.	Z24: Reasonable arrangement of students' work and rest schedule.	
	Reasonable arrangement of rich curriculum teaching activities.	Z25: Ensure students' off-line autonomous learning time.	
	It is suggested to adopt the form of "Live Broadcast + Resource Package".		
Ga10	Choose high-quality teaching resources to push to students.	Z26: Provide high-quality teaching resources.	
	Pay attention to stimulate students' interest in learning.	Z27: Actively mobilize students' initiative, initiative, and creativity in learning.	
	Pay attention to students' online learning in real time.	Z28: Monitor students' online learning.	

Coding Number	Original Statement	Conceptualization	Category
Ga11	Coordinated organization and promotion, the city as a whole to play "A game of chess". Implement strategies according to different levels in order to make the learning section "A line". Efficiently organize teaching to make online school be like "One kind". Gather the resources of famous teachers, quality control like "A Chain". Teaching and research guidance in place, evaluation and improvement "Integration". Strengthen supervision and management, resolutely prevent to be like "Swarm".	Z29: Grasp the overall requirements of teaching, overall planning and adjust measures to local conditions. Z30: Construction of high-quality teaching resource bank for local autonomous choice. Z31: Observe and evaluate teachers' teaching work according to normal teaching. Z32: Strengthen the course audit and online teaching process supervision.	
Ga12	Family education micro-lecture meets different learning needs. Provide a variety of online help for students who are about to enter school. Take online teaching to ensure that "Class will not be suspended".	Z33: Guide parents to familiarize themselves with the process of "Disrupted Classes, Undisrupted Learning". Z34: Provide varied online help for students who are about to enter school. Z35: Take online teaching to ensure "Disrupted Classes, Undisrupted Learning".	

(*Continued*)

Table B1 Examples of open coding and axial coding of policy

Coding Number	Original Statement	Conceptualization	Category
Ga13	Guide students to carry out autonomous learning.	Z36: Cultivate students' autonomous learning ability.	
	Reasonable allocation of "Teaching" and "Learning" time.	Z37: Reasonable arrangement of students' work and rest schedule.	
	Stimulate students' sense of responsibility, urgency and initiative in learning.	Z38: Actively mobilize students' initiative, initiative, and creativity in learning.	
	Online teaching must abandon the one-way indoctrination of teachers' long-time teaching.	Z39: Choose different teaching plans according to different students' learning needs.	
	Pay attention to the design of teaching content, which should be combined with epidemic prevention and control.		
	Choose appropriate online teaching forms.		
Ga14	Integrate high-quality teaching resources.	Z40: Provide high-quality teaching resources.	
	Pay attention to the online interaction between teachers and students;	Z41: Be responsible for daily contact and guiding students' study at home.	
	The online teaching service should be based on the principle of autonomous learning as the main part and online classroom live broadcast as the auxiliary part.	Z42: Avoid increasing unnecessary burdens on students.	
	The proper amount of homework, an appropriate layout, and timely feedback are the three guarantees for the effectiveness of homework after online teaching.		
	It is not permitted to increase students' schoolwork burden.		

(Continued)

Coding Number	Original Statement	Conceptualization	Category
Ga15	The teaching and research groups of various disciplines in the school still need to carry out school-based teaching and research based on the network, plan the teaching arrangement of students' home-based learning as a whole, collect the curriculum resources that can be used for reference, discuss and design learning tasks that can promote students' learning, and arrange the teaching management of students' home-based learning as a whole.	Z43: Make an overall adjustment to teaching arrangements.	
Ga16	Set up a psychological lecturer group and carry out a psychological micro-class. Set up a public welfare lecturer group to carry out a public welfare micro class; Set up a student lecturer group and carry out a professional micro class.	Z44: Pay attention to students' mental health. Z45: Pay attention to the public welfare of teaching resources.	
Ga17	In order to further enrich platform resources and promote the all-round development of students, the Ministry of Education upgraded the platform and added primary school, junior high school, and ordinary senior high school courses to be broadcast by CETV4. Students can watch live TV through the platform or watch it on demand in the course learning column.	Z46: Provide free network platforms for local schools to use independently.	

Table B1 Examples of open coding and axial coding of policy

Coding Number	Original Statement	Conceptualization	Category
Ga18	"Classroom in the Cloud" "Online Learning" The Ezhou Municipal Bureau of Education formulated the implementation plan and clearly issued the teaching requirements of "Four Focuses". First, pay attention to the cultivation of autonomous learning ability. Each school should formulate a flexible, scientific, and reasonable schedule and curriculum, to ensure that students have enough time for autonomous learning. High school and junior high school students make their own learning plans, and primary school students engage in autonomous learning under the guidance of teachers and parents. Second, focus on cultivating students' core literacy. In the teaching content, carry out "Five education simultaneously", focus on strengthening the education of patriotism and socialist core values, infiltrate the education of rule of law, environmental protection, integrity, and responsibility, and cultivate students' good behavior habits. Third, pay attention to life safety and mental health education. Teach the first lesson of safety education well, treat epidemic prevention and control as a textbook, and put epidemic prevention knowledge and safety education throughout the whole process of home learning. Fourth, pay attention to improving the mechanism of home-school joint education. Seize the opportunity of home isolation; teachers should strengthen communication with parents, provide mutual support and cooperation, and lay the foundation for students' work after returning to school.	Z47: Cultivate students' autonomous learning ability. Z48: Cultivate students' core quality. Z49: Focus on life safety and mental health education. Z50: Family-school cooperation.	

(Continued)

Coding Number	Original Statement	Conceptualization	Category
Ga19	In terms of learning style, the local government respected the objective reality and gives students "Various Choices" according to local conditions. They can choose the most suitable learning style for children. A TV, computer, tablet, or mobile phone can be used as a learning device. In order to ensure the quality of teaching, all schools in the city set up subject network teaching and research groups to actively carry out teaching and research exchanges, learn from strong points to make up for their own weak points, select personalized online teaching methods, and guide students' study and life during the anti-epidemic period.	Z51: Grasp the overall requirements of teaching, overall planning, suit measures to local conditions. Z52: The online learning of junior students can be chosen voluntarily under the guidance of parents.	
Ga20	Mobilize the city's famous teachers, key teachers, and discipline leaders to form a "Excellent Class" team, focusing on 20 topics such as "Epidemic prevention and control, habit formation, extracurricular reading, home exercise, and social practice", with each person giving at least two "Excellent Classes", which will be broadcast directly to the city's primary and secondary school students, so as to realize the "Full Coverage" of rural remote schools and weak schools. On this basis, open up information resources in an all-around way, relying on synchronous classrooms, TV synchronous teaching, the Hubei Education cloud, central video, and etc., and establish an online teaching resources supermarket for teachers to choose from.	Z53: Set up a teachers' research group. Z54: Create excellent online teaching resources.	

Table B1 Examples of open coding and axial coding of policy

Coding Number	Original Statement	Conceptualization	Category
Ga21	Use the "Famous Teacher Studio" to carry out training and guidance, reply online to teachers' questions more than 7,000 times, and greatly improve the operation ability of rural teachers using information means of teaching.	Z55: Improve rural teachers' information teaching ability.	
Ga22	Teachers are required to design coaching exercises every day to guide students to think independently, ask questions, and resolve doubts immediately, accurately analyze students' learning situation, and formulate weekly teaching plans. Teachers should carry out "One-to-One" guidance and help for children left behind, disabled children, and students from poor families, so as to let the sunshine of online teaching shine on every child.	Z56: Guide students to think independently Z57: Analyze students' learning and make weekly teaching plan. Z58: "One to One" help for students of special groups.	
Ga23	In principle, the progress of online teaching should not exceed half of that of normal classroom teaching. A reasonable arrangement of online centralized teaching and off-line autonomous learning content, overall control of learning intensity, and the amount of homework. Do not increase the burden of students' schoolwork. See that every student can watch it as the starting point. Even if the course is broadcast live, it is necessary to provide video courses for students to choose from and fully consider the particularity of students and their families.	Z59: Improve online teaching methods. Z60: Avoid increasing unnecessary burdens on students.	

Coding Number	Original Statement	Conceptualization	Category
Ga24	A scientific and reasonable grasp of online learning time, according to the requirements of the implementation of different periods of online time. In primary school, every period should be about 20 minutes, and in middle school, every period should be about 30 minutes, recess time not less than 15 minutes, and eyesight exercises and recess activities should be arranged.	Z61: Strictly control online learning time.	
Ga25	Implement the unified curriculum arranged by the Education Bureau and arrange homework help and other follow-up work in the independent time period of the school, so as to make it clear day by day. At the same time, according to the actual situation of each year, the corresponding homework requirements are issued, in which there is no homework in grade one and grade two of primary school. Sports and art courses are pushed once a week in the form of task list, which does not occupy the time for independent arrangements. Students are mainly flexible and independent, and videos or pictures are pushed once a week at most.	Z62: Standardize curriculum management.	
Ga26	Around the overall curriculum resources of the epidemic situation, the project-based learning content of each period is formulated and actively organized to ensure that all teachers design and all students participate. Actively carry out reading guidance, labor practice, knowledge carding, and other open-learning activities.	Z63: Actively carry out project-based learning.	

(Continued)

Table B1 Examples of open coding and axial coding of policy

Coding Number	Original Statement	Conceptualization	Category
Ga27	Fully open online live teaching: adhere to the six sections of "Unified arrangement, unified strategy, unified class hours, unified content, unified requirements, and unified guidance", and do not implement "One size fits all" for the online teaching platform, teaching content, curriculum arrangement, or organizational form. The Xianyang Municipal Bureau of education should fully deploy, promote, and establish an operational mechanism for collaborative promotion. Set up a leading group for online teaching work, which includes organizing teacher training, strengthening online teaching guidance, making good use of network resources, and establishing a special maintenance team to promote online teaching work. Integrate the city's teaching staff, high-quality digital resources, and a high-quality online education platform to carry out online education and teaching activities. Public welfare "Cloud Classroom" solution.	Z64: Fully open online live teaching. Z65: Overall planning and adjusting measures to local conditions. Z66: Strengthen teachers' information teaching training. Z67: Integrate high-quality teaching resources. Z68: Focus on public welfare. Z69: Focus on home-school communication.	
Ga28	In order to ensure the quality of online teaching, the school-based network teaching platform, Superstar, Love Course, Wisdom Tree, Rain Classroom, and other internal and external curriculum resources and platforms are integrated as a whole. Teachers are organized to do a good job in online lesson preparation in advance, carry out online teaching training for teachers, and carry out teaching activities such as recording and broadcasting teaching, synchronous classrooms, and teaching interaction on the platform.	Z70: Overall planning and integration of school-based network teaching platform. Z71: Organize teachers to prepare lessons. Z72: Develop online teaching training for teachers.	

Coding Number	Original Statement	Conceptualization	Category
Ga29	Effectively promote the construction and application of online courses, so the average attendance rate of students reaches 96.65%. The online interaction between teachers and students is good, which changes the teaching and learning concept of teachers and students. The school also does a good job in guaranteeing real-time network service, establishes the course center service group and school live room training, improves the online teaching monitoring mechanism, organizes experts to listen to and evaluate courses online, and ensures the homogeneity and equivalence of online learning and off-line classroom teaching.	Z73: Good interactions between teachers and students. Z74: Change the teaching and learning concepts of teachers and students. Z75: Real time network service guarantee. Z76: Establish online supervision mechanism for online courses.	
Ga30	The university will also build 15 online open courses on the platforms of MOOC, Xuetang online, Wisdom Tree, etc., which are open to teachers and students of colleges and universities and the public free of charge.	Z77: Free online courses for the public.	

In order to identify the relationship between the initial concept and category, determine the main and secondary categories, use the combination of qualitative and quantitative methods to encode the principal axis, and calculate the percentage of each initial concept in the total number of samples, as shown in Table B2.

Table B2 The percentage of the initial concepts in the total sample numbers

Concept Number	Concept Name	Percentage (%)	Concept Number	Concept Name	Percentage (%)
Z1	Carry out online teaching	63.33	Z25	The arrangement of online courses should be consistent with the school as far as possible	26.67
Z2	Do a good job of post-school teaching and learning at home	10	Z26	Avoid adding unnecessary burden to students	16.67
Z3	Carry out education activities related to epidemic situation	30	Z27	Pay attention to the problem of students' eyesight	30
Z4	Overall adjustment of teaching arrangement	13.33	Z28	Arrange a reasonable schedule for students	23.33
Z5	Special help for special groups	10	Z29	Strengthen the psychological guidance of students	13.33
Z6	Strengthen the guidance and supervision of the e-learning space	6.67	Z30	Pay attention to the cultivation of students' awareness and ability of autonomous learning	30
Z7	Guide parents to control their children's time spent looking at electronic products	10	Z31	Actively mobilize students' learning active, initiative, and creativity	10
Z8	Strengthen the training and guidance of teachers' information technology teaching ability	36.67	Z32	Monitor the online learning of students	16.67
Z9	Encourage the team of expert teachers to develop high-quality teaching curriculum resources	13.33	Z33	The construction of high-quality teaching resource database for local autonomous choice	50
Z10	Strengthen the cultivation of network teaching ability of teachers	16.67	Z34	Related enterprises provide network technology support	20

(Continued)

Table B2 (Continued) The percentage of the initial concepts in the total sample numbers

Concept Number	Concept Name	Percentage (%)	Concept Number	Concept Name	Percentage (%)
Z11	Improve teachers' ability to use high-quality network teaching platform and resources to carry out teaching	10	Z35	Provide a free network platform for independent use of each school	30
Z12	Promote the teaching organization at the grassroots level and carry out online teaching and research activities	6.67	Z36	Adhere to the public welfare of network courses and network teaching resources	16.67
Z13	Encourage the team of expert teachers to develop high-quality teaching curriculum resources	9.68	Z37	To provide teachers with information-based teaching related training	33.33
Z14	Strengthen the network teaching ability training of teachers	19.35	Z38	Provide high-quality teaching resources and the use of network live platform	10
Z15	Improve teachers' ability to use high-quality network teaching platform and resources to carry out teaching	16.13	Z39	Guide parents to master online learning methods	20
Z16	Promote the teaching organization at the grassroots level and carry out online teaching and research activities	9.68	Z40	Adhere to the combination of curriculum learning and epidemic prevention and control knowledge learning	30
Z17	Online teaching and online lesson preparation	50	Z41	Strengthen the interaction with teachers online	20
Z18	Choose the teaching mode independently according to the region and period	16.67	Z42	Choose the appropriate way of learning for autonomous learning	30
Z19	According to the learning needs of students to choose teaching programs	6.67	Z43	Guide parents to control the use time of children's electronic products	20

Concept Number	Concept Name	Percentage (%)	Concept Number	Concept Name	Percentage (%)
Z20	Teachers' online teaching workload is counted as performance	16.67	**Z44**	Accompany junior students in online classes	20
Z21	Inspect and evaluate teachers' teaching work according to normal teaching	10	**Z45**	Parents should guide and voluntarily choose the length of online learning in lower grades	16.67
Z22	Teachers provide help and feedback to students immediately	26.67	**Z46**	Parents take the initiative to familiarize themselves with online learning methods in advance	13.33
Z23	Strengthen the course audit and online teaching process supervision	20			
Z24	The time limit stipulates the study time of students in different periods	30			

Through the analysis of the overall data in Table B2, initial concepts that account for less than 20% are eliminated or integrated. Thus, the coding table of government entities with 20 countermeasures is obtained, as shown in Table B3.

Table B3 Coding table of the exploratory period of the government

Subject	Level	Countermeasure	Child Countermeasure	Proportion (%)
Schools	Organizations' Level	Deployment of the preparatory work of "Disrupted Class, Undisrupted Learning"	Develop network course teaching	63.33
			Do a good job in the connection of teaching and home learning after the beginning of school	10
			Carry out educational activities related to the epidemic situation	30
			Adjust the teaching arrangement as a whole	13.33
			Provide special help to special groups	10
		Strengthen the cooperation between families and schools	Guide parents to accept and master online learning methods in advance	10
			Strengthen the guidance and supervision of online learning	6.67
			Guide parents to control their children's spending on electronic products	10
	Teachers' Level	Support the training and cooperation of teachers to improve their information teaching level	Strengthen the training and guidance of teachers' information technology teaching ability	36.67
			Encourage teams of expert teachers to develop high-quality teaching curriculum resources	13.33
			Strengthen the cultivation of network teaching ability of teachers	16.67
			Improve the ability of teachers to use high-quality network teaching platforms and resources to carry out teaching	10
			Promote grass-roots teaching organizations to carry out online teaching and research activities	6.67

(Continued)

Table B3 Coding table of the exploratory period of the government

Subject	Level	Countermeasure	Child Countermeasure	Proportion (%)
		Encourage teachers to adopt effective teaching methods	Online teaching and online lesson preparation	50
			Choose the teaching mode independently according to different regions and stages	16.67
			Choose teaching plan according to students' learning needs	6.67
		Improve the monitoring mechanism of online teaching to ensure the quality of teaching	Teachers' online teaching workload should be included in performance	16.67
			Investigate and evaluate teachers' teaching work according to normal teaching	10
			Teachers ought to provide help and feedback to students immediately	26.67
			Strengthen the course audit and online teaching process supervision	20
		Pay attention to the burden of students' online learning	The time limit for students to study in different classes was stipulated	30
			The arrangement of online courses should be consistent with the schools as far as possible	26.67
			Avoid adding unnecessary burdens to students	16.67
	Students' Level	Pay attention to students' physical and mental health	Pay attention to students' eyesight	30
			Reasonable arrangement of students' schedule	23.33
			Strengthen students' psychological guidance	13.33
		Cultivate students' autonomous learning ability	Pay attention to the cultivation of students' awareness and ability of autonomous learning	30
			Actively mobilize students' activity, initiative and creativity in learning	10
			Monitor the online learning of students	16.67

Subject	Level	Countermeasure	Child Countermeasure	Proportion (%)
Enterprises	Organizations' Level	Provide technical resources support for a wide range of "Disrupted Class, Undisrupted Learning" activities	Build a high-quality teaching resource library for local autonomous choice	50
			Related enterprises provide network technology support	20
			Provide free network platforms for each school to use independently	30
	Teachers' Level	Adhere to the public beneficial of network courses and network teaching resources		16.67
		Provide training related to information teaching for teachers		33.33
	Students' Level	Provide high-quality learning resources and the instructions of webcast platforms		10
	Families' Level	Guide parents to master online learning methods		20
Families	Advice for students	Adhere to the combination of curriculum learning and knowledge learning of epidemic prevention and control		30
		Strengthen the interaction with teachers online		20
		Choose an appropriate way of learning and study independently		30
	Advice for parents	Guide parents to control the use time of children's electronic products		20
		Accompany junior students in class		20
		Parents voluntarily choose the length of online learning for the lower grades		16.67
		Parents took the initiative to get familiar with online learning methods in advance		13.33

C Appendix C. Coding process table of the fully deployed period of the government

Combined with the coding mode of the government entities in the third stage of the fully deployed period in the 2.4 coding scheme, this section carries out three rounds of coding: open coding, principal axis coding, and selection coding. The coding results are shown in Tables C1–C3.

Table C1 Examples of open coding and axial coding of policy

Coding Number	Original Statement	Conceptualization	Category
Ga1	Famous teacher team had built high-quality courses, and teachers had trained online education and teaching-related information technology capabilities, and carried out the special education of "practicing contract, self-discipline and self-study" to students by using the network. "One school, one policy" should teach students in accordance with their aptitude, coordinate the city's network resources, and ensure the operating environment of relevant platforms, cloud services, and network information security, and organize all operators to cooperate to ensure the smooth distribution of teaching content and interactive channels, and strive to create an "air classroom" covering all primary and secondary school students.	Z1: Provide high-quality online education and teaching resources Z2: Training teachers' information teaching ability	ZZ1: Make emergency plan by various forces ZZ2: Adhere to public welfare ZZ3: Carry out education activities related to the epidemic situation ZZ4: Improve the monitoring mechanism of online teaching to ensure the quality of teaching
Ga2	Watching the uniformly recorded video courses could share high-quality resources in the whole city, and the management and interaction of different classes could give full play to the positive role of the original school, the original class, and the original subordinate teachers, and strive to achieve the effect of "simple, reliable, stable, and minimum". Among them, the district undertook the main responsibility of building a teacher-student interaction platform, and the school undertook the main responsibility of ensuring the quality of teaching. The Air Studio Class emphasizes "full coverage". Online education this time emphasizes that it should cover every student and never let any student fall behind.	Z3: Arrange teaching according to the actual situation Z4: Make full use of high-quality teaching resources Z5: Optimize the communication link of teaching interaction Z6: Ensure full coverage of online learning Z7: Provide a guarantee of network technology Z8: Reduce the burden on parents and students	ZZ5: Pay attention to the problem of students' network learning burden ZZ6: Pay attention to physical and mental health ZZ7: Strengthen the interaction between home and school

(Continued)

Table C1 Examples of open coding and axial coding of policy

Coding Number	Original Statement	Conceptualization	Category
Ga3	On the first day of the "online class", Yang Youjie, deputy director of the school running, and Mr. Liu Peng, deputy director of the party office, respectively presented lectures on "New Coronavirus pneumonia prevention and control" and "Practicing the socialist core values -- gathering the positive energy of youth". On the morning of March 3, 2020, according to the plan of online teaching, the first lesson of the school's "online classroom" was a complete success. The teachers have mastered the operation method of online live course, and the students have gradually adapted to the form of online lectures. They listen carefully and interact actively, forming a good atmosphere, which is highly praised by the students and their parents.	Z9: Arrange teaching activities related to epidemic situation Z10: Training teachers' ability of information teaching Z11: Create a good learning atmosphere	ZZ8: Support teacher training and collaboration ZZ9: Collect opinions from teachers, students, and parents ZZ10: Pay attention to the burden of e-learning ZZ11: Teachers should pay attention to improving their own information teaching level ZZ12: Take effective teaching methods ZZ13: Strengthen the classified guidance and education for students ZZ14: Investigate the online learning situation of students ZZ15: Guide students to make study plans at home

(Continued)

Coding Number	Original Statement	Conceptualization	Category
Ga4	The school would solicit the opinions of teachers and students from various channels, further optimize the online teaching scheme, ensure the orderly development of online teaching, and prepare for the off-line classroom teaching after returning to school. It provided PPT, teaching video, homework, discussion and other resources with UMOOC platform before class to organize students to learn. In the classroom, the Tencent classroom, ZOOM, Ding Ding, QQ group, Rain classroom, classroom group, and other platforms were combined to conduct the live broadcast and interaction of the course. After class, homework submission, question answering, and course feedback are carried out through UMOOC and other platforms.	Z12: Collect the opinions of teachers and students from many aspects Z13: Do a good job in the connection between online teaching and off-line teaching after the beginning of school Z14: Make full use of high-quality network teaching platform Z15: Provide high-quality network teaching resources	
Ga5	In order to improve the learning effect of students, teachers also provide students with better teaching resources through the exploration of the national professional teaching resources library, online courses of the Vocational and Technical Education Institute launched by Guangdong Provincial Education Department, a network collective preparation platform for ideological and political teachers in national universities, an online open curriculum alliance platform of universities in the Dawan district, Guangdong, Hong Kong, and Macao, and a public class platform of the people's network Rich learning resource. The school also organized and carried out diversified and targeted online education, strengthened classified guidance and education for students of different grades and majors, and actively cooperated with enterprises to carry out online teaching.	Z16: Strengthen classified guidance and education for students Z17: Encourage schools to actively cooperate with enterprises	

Table C1 Examples of open coding and axial coding of policy

Coding Number	Original Statement	Conceptualization	Category
Ga6	Adhere to integrated promotion, fully implement network teaching for the primary and secondary schools in the city, realize "stop teaching, stop teaching, Disrupted Class, Undisrupted Learning," of the primary and secondary schools in the city, and adhere to multiplatform development. In addition to making good use of the provincial "zhi jiang hui" and the municipal "Bawu school", all counties (cities, districts) and schools, in combination with local realities, make full use of multiple channels such as "Hua shu", mobile, telecom, linkage, and "DingDing" to build learning platforms.	Z18: Insist on carrying out network teaching in an all-around way Z19: Adhere to a variety of learning platforms to carry out online learning	
Ga7	Adhere to the implementation of standardization. It should standardize the teaching content, arrange the teaching plan and schedule according to the teaching needs of different periods and disciplines, standardize teaching time, and strictly control the time of online teaching courses.	Z20: Adhere to the standardization of teaching content and teaching time	
Ga8	Adhere to the promotion of public welfare. Online teaching clearly "zero charge"; schools and training institutions were strictly prohibited to charge parents and students in any form.	Z21: Adhere to the public welfare promotion of network courses	
Ga9	The Department of Education of Guangdong Province, through the online open course alliance of colleges and universities in Guangdong, Hong Kong, and Macao, provides technical support for the online education of undergraduate colleges and universities in Guangdong Province. The guidance alliance invites famous teachers and the person in charge of national excellent online open courses, and carries out two phases of the live sharing of excellent online teaching cases, so as to help teachers change their roles as soon as possible and improve the level of online teaching.	Z22: Provide high-quality network teaching resources Z23: Provide network technology support	

(*Continued*)

Coding Number	Original Statement	Conceptualization	Category
Ga10	To formulate the implementation guide of online teaching in this professional field, provide a list of high-quality online courses in this professional field, and publish the guide and list on the portal platform of online open course alliance of colleges and universities in Guangdong, Hong Kong, and Macao Dawan District, so as to provide teachers with learning and references.	Z24: Provide experience for teachers Z25: Improve teachers' skills in software operation	
Ga11	Taking advantage of the professional advantages of the provincial education technology and Education Commission, the "comparison and recommendation of online teaching live platform function test" was released to help teachers understand the basic performance of each online teaching platform and facilitate teachers' scientific selection; at the same time, it had developed and completed the website "special forum on improving teachers' online teaching ability", which helps teachers to do a good job in the service exchange and guarantee of opening, selecting and using courses, and answering questions online in a timely manner.	Z26: Optimize the link of teaching interaction and communication Z27: Ensure timely reply to the students' confusion	
Ga12	The content involves the caliber of prevention and control work, teachers' online training, curriculum resources release, curriculum construction requirements, stress testing, and other aspects. It is necessary to clarify the relevant requirements of online teaching, guide colleges and universities to take a good direction, and steadily promote teaching.	Z28: Train teachers' to improve their ability in information teaching	

Table C1 Examples of open coding and axial coding of policy

Coding Number	Original Statement	Conceptualization	Category
Ga13	Under the framework of the overall plan of the university, it guides the colleges and universities in the city to continuously improve the online teaching plan, reasonably adjust and arrange the teaching plans for spring and autumn semester courses, coordinate the teaching arrangements of undergraduate, graduate, higher vocational and continuing education, and clarify the relevant requirements for key links such as registration, retirement, and re-election, make-up examinations, minors, online teaching, practice, and so on, to find the node of time.	Z29: Clarify the requirements of online teaching Z30: Do a good job in the connection between online teaching and off-line teaching after the beginning of school Z31: Arrange teaching according to the actual situation	
Ga14	The Municipal Education Commission builds and information and resource release and sharing platform for colleges and universities. Promptly forward the relevant document requirements of the Higher Education Department of the Ministry of Education on the organization and management of online teaching, and recommend 24,000 high-quality online courses and more than 2,000 virtual simulation experiment courses of the national virtual simulation experiment teaching project sharing platform of dozens of free online course platforms organized by the Ministry of Education. At the same time, this book also use the online course resources of "Shanghai University Ideological and political theory course online course platform" to publish and recommend municipal demonstration ideological and political courses, and organize excellent teachers to shoot the teaching videos of "computer application foundation" and "College English" in higher vocational colleges, which greatly enriches the online course resources of colleges and universities in our city.	Z32: Provide high-quality network teaching resources	

(Continued)

Coding Number	Original Statement	Conceptualization	Category
Ga15	Organize online teaching case collection, collect typical experiences, outstanding deeds and touching stories during online teaching. Organize video conferences and on-site seminars on online teaching for undergraduates, postgraduates, higher vocational colleges, and continuing education to exchange and share experiences and practices in promoting online teaching.	Z33: Provide teachers with typical teaching case experience	
Ga16	The "Cloud classroom" breaks the traditional teaching mode and extends the learning scene from off-line to online, which is a test for both teachers and students. Therefore, many colleges and universities are arranged in advance, and teachers prepare in advance and try to present ideal online classroom for students. The teachers of the Guangzhou International Campus of South China University of Technology "all out" shock training, learning the use of live platform software, purchasing network equipment and information, carefully prepared a number of teaching programs. According to the introduction, the "cloud classroom" of the Wu Xianming School of Intelligent Engineering adheres to all English teaching. Teachers and students adopt the form of "teaching video + cloud class + QQ group". The interaction between teachers and students was warm and smooth, the classroom content was rich, and students' thinking was fully mobilized.	Z34: Reasonable arrangement of online teaching Z35: Make full use of high-quality network teaching platform Z36: Improving teachers' software operation skills	

Table C1 Examples of open coding and axial coding of policy

Coding Number	Original Statement	Conceptualization	Category
Ga17	In these online courses, Huanong plans to use multiple public MOOCS platforms, multiple online live broadcast platforms and the "education online" platform on campus to teach, so as to prevent the network congestion of teaching platforms due to the centralized online opening of schools in many places across the country. Yuan Bing, a teacher of the school of civil and traffic engineering, and the teaching team together create an online course of structural mechanics for students, which turns the traditional classroom into a flipped classroom of online experiments.	Z37: Ensure sufficient network equipment and information Z38: Optimize the link of teaching interaction and communication	
Ga18	In the actual implementation of the course, due to some network problems such as stuck, can timely use the backup scheme, change the network platform, and other ways to successfully complete the teaching. Liu Minggui, Secretary of the Party committee of Lingnan Normal University, and LAN Yanze, President of Lingnan Normal University, carefully prepared the online teaching content of "the first lesson of Ideological and political education" for the students, exchanged their thinking experience and action harvest of epidemic prevention and control, and gathered the spiritual strength of working together in the same boat to overcome the difficulties.	Z39: Provide network technical support Z40: Arrange teaching activities related to the epidemic situation	

Coding Number	Original Statement	Conceptualization	Category
Ga19	"Online class" arrangement in place. In Wenzhou City, we took the lead in formulating the implementation plan of "air classroom" for the extended opening of primary and secondary schools in Yueqing City. The first period was February 9–17, 2020, the second period was February 20–28, 2020, and the third period was March 3–15, 2020. It organized more than 200 famous and excellent teachers, opened 12 subjects, and had more than 600 class hours. During the compulsory education stage, more than 100,000 students from Grade 4 to Grade 9 participated in live learning through the Internet and Huashu TV.	Z41: Provide sufficient high-quality network teaching resources Z42: Provide a variety of online learning methods	
Ga20	So far, more than 50 million people have visited six live broadcast sites. At the same time, "suggestions on life and study guidance for Grades 1–3 of Yueqing primary school in winter vacation" and "tips on education work during delayed opening of Yueqing kindergartens" were formulated and make full use of the high-quality resources of the famous head teacher's studio, online launched for Grades 1 to 6 "war" epidemic "micro class meeting, adhere to a daily update, has been even more 42 days. Preparations for the start of the school are in place. Scientifically adjust the overall teaching plan for the first half of the year, standardize the setting of temporary isolation points, and actively make preparations for epidemic prevention materials.	Z43: Guarantee the full coverage of online learning Z44: Make full use of high-quality teaching resources Z45: Do a good job in the connection between online teaching and off-line teaching after the beginning of school	

In order to find the relationship between the initial concept and category, determine the main and secondary categories, use the combination of qualitative and quantitative methods to encode the principal axis, and calculate the percentage of each initial concept in the total number of samples, as shown in Table C2.

Table C2 The percentage of the initial concepts in the total sample numbers

Concept Number	Concept Name	Percentage (%)	Concept Number	Concept Name	Percentage (%)
Z1	Do a good job in the connection of teaching and home learning after the beginning of school	10	Z17	Avoid adding unnecessary burden to students	13.33
Z2	Carry out education activities related to the epidemic situation	26.67	Z18	Pay attention to the problem of students' eyesight	6.67
Z3	According to the actual situation to arrange related teaching activities	43.33	Z19	It is necessary to arrange students' work and rest schedule reasonably	13.33
Z4	Special help for special groups	10	Z20	Strengthen the psychological guidance of students	16.67
Z5	Strengthen the cooperation between family and school	23.33	Z21	Strengthen the classified guidance and education for students	16.67
Z6	Strengthen the training and guidance of teachers' information technology teaching ability	40	Z22	Survey students' online learning	10
Z7	Strengthen the cultivation of network teaching ability of teachers	40	Z23	Guide students to make home study plan	13.33
Z8	Improve teachers' ability to use high-quality network teaching platform and resources to carry out teaching	16.67	Z24	Build a high-quality teaching resource bank for local autonomous choice	33.33
Z9	Provide typical case experience for teachers	10	Z25	Provide subsidies for network traffic	6.67
Z10	Make full use of high-quality network teaching resources and platforms	16.67	Z26	Relevant enterprises need to provide network technology support	36.67
Z11	Optimize the communication link of teaching interaction	20	Z27	Provide free network platform for schools to use independently	6.67
Z12	Provide homework answer in time	40	Z28	Adhere to the public welfare of network courses and network teaching resources	10

(Continued)

Table C2 (Continued) The percentage of the initial concepts in the total sample numbers

Concept Number	Concept Name	Percentage (%)	Concept Number	Concept Name	Percentage (%)
Z13	Teachers' online teaching workload is counted as performance	6.67	**Z29**	It is necessary to provide teachers with information-based teaching related training	40
Z14	Strengthen the supervision of course audit and online teaching process	20	**Z30**	Provide high-quality teaching resources and the use of network live platform	10
Z15	Collect opinions among teachers, students and parents from a wide range	20	**Z31**	Guide parents to master online learning methods	6.67
Z16	The arrangement of online courses should be consistent with the school as far as possible	10			

Through the analysis of the overall data in Table C2, the initial concepts that account for less than 20% are eliminated or integrated. Thus, the coding table of the government subject with 15 countermeasures is obtained, as shown in Table C3.

Table C3 Coding table of the fully deployed period of the government

Subject	Level	Countermeasure	Child Countermeasure	Proportion
Schools	Organizations' Level		Link teaching and home learning after the term started	10
			Carry out educational activities related to the COVID-19	26.67
			Arrange teaching activities based on the actual situation	43.33
			Offer special assistant for disadvantaged groups	10
		Strengthen the cooperation between families and schools		23.33
	Teachers' Level	Support the skill training and internal collaboration of teachers to improve their information technology instruction	Enhance the training and guidance of teachers' information technology instruction	40
			Advance the cultivation of online teaching ability of teachers	40
			Improve the teachers' competence of carrying out teaching activities by online teaching platforms and resources of high-quality	16.67
			Provide typical cases for teachers to refer to	10
		Encourage teachers to adopt effective teaching methods	Use high-class online teaching resources and platforms to full advantage	16.67
			Optimize the link of teaching interaction	20
			Offer timely Q&A of assignment	40
		Perfect the online-teaching monitoring mechanism to ensure the teaching quality	Calculate the teachers' online workload into the performance	6.67
			Tighter process regulation of curriculum review and online teaching	20
		Gather opinions among teachers, students, and parents from a wide range		20
		Focus on students' burden in online study	The arrangement of online courses is consistent with off-line courses	10
			Avoid the unnecessary burdens of students	13.33

Subject	Level	Countermeasure	Child Countermeasure	Proportion
	Students' Level	Attach great importance to students' physical and mental health	Emphasis students' eyesight issues	6.67
			Schedule students' time reasonably	13.33
			Intensify the psychological counsel of students	16.67
		Reinforce the classified guidance to students		16.67
		Investigate students' learning		10
		Instruct students to make the online-study plan		13.33
Enterprises	Organizations' Level	Provide technical resources for the widespread activity of "Disrupted Class, Undisrupted Learning"	Develop the excellent education resources for local independent choices	33.33
			Subsidize the network flow	6.67
			Technical guarantee offered by related enterprises	36.67
			Provide free online platform for local schools to use independently	6.67
		Insist on the public welfare of courses and education resources		10
	Teachers' Level	Supply training sessions of informational teaching for teachers		40
	Students' Level	Give high-quality education resources and the methods of webcast platform		10
	Families' Level	Conduct parents to master the procedure of online learning		6.67

D Appendix D. Coding process table of the exiting period of the government

Combined with the coding mode of the government entities in the third stage of the exiting period in 2.4 coding scheme, this paper carries out three rounds of coding according to the open coding, principal axis coding and selection coding. The coding results are shown in Tables D1–D3.

Table D1 Examples of open coding and axial coding of policy

Coding Number	Original Statement	Conceptualization	Category
Ga1	In order to make the connection between online and off-line teaching more targeted, the Academy of education and Sciences of Weifang High tech Zone began to conduct an investigation in March. By means of questionnaire, online testing, and thousands of teachers' cloud visits to thousands of homes, it organizes primary and secondary schools in the whole region to comprehensively understand the students' online learning situation, guides schools to formulate off-line and online teaching connection plans, optimizes subject teaching plans, reasonably arranges teaching progress, and "one school, one plan" completes the connection work.	Z1: Issue notice of resumption of classes Z2: Overall adjustment of teaching arrangement	ZZ1: Emergency plan for epidemic prevention in Campus ZZ2: Make overall arrangements for epidemic prevention and protection in schools of all levels and types ZZ3: Effectively carry out the transformation between online teaching and off-line Teaching ZZ4: Do a good job of psychological guidance for students
Ga2	Weifang High Tech Bilingual School released a letter to parents through parents' WeChat group in spring and related work arrangements at the beginning of the school, guiding parents to urge their children to prepare personal protective equipment for the beginning of the school, and sorting out online study notes and homework. Gangcheng modern school further strengthens class management and psychological counseling, carries out self-discipline education activities in the form of online theme class meeting, and effectively supervises and regulates students' learning state in various ways.	Z3: To guide the scientific formulation of the program for the connection of returning to school and returning to classes Z4: Teachers should adjust the curriculum Z5: Guiding students to adjust their psychology Z6: Guide students to pay attention to their daily protection	ZZ5: Pay attention to physical and mental health ZZ6: Guiding students to adjust their psychology ZZ7: Guide students to pay attention to their daily protection ZZ8: Guide the scientific formulation of the connection scheme of returning to school and returning to class teaching ZZ9: Guide students to develop the awareness of daily epidemic prevention

(Continued)

Table D1 (Continued) Examples of open coding and axial coding of policy

Coding Number	Original Statement	Conceptualization	Category
Ga3	The quality and learning effect of online public welfare classroom was the focus of parents and students. Through the online collective lesson preparation and grinding, the teaching and research staff of Weifang High tech Zone Academy of Educational Sciences carry out the education plan training and guidance of pre class preview plan, in class learning plan and after class homework plan from the regional level. Yang Shuping, President of Weifang High tech Zone Institute of education and science, said that the teaching and research staff of various disciplines spend half a day every week to carry out network teaching and research in different grades, and conduct collective discussion on the design of preview tasks, the guidance of learning activities, and the assignment of assignments.	Z7:Effectively carry out the transformation between online teaching and off-line Teaching	ZZ10: Guiding students to adjust their psychology ZZ11: Strengthen the management of teaching service and attach importance to the guidance of students' mental health ZZ12: Enterprises provide guidance on the connection between the resumption of classes and online learning ZZ13: Hold lectures and forums for front-line teachers to provide effective conversion between off-line teaching and online teaching ZZ14: Provide parents with relevant information on how to resume school through official account, etc. ZZ15: Parents should guide students to adjust their psychology

Coding Number	Original Statement	Conceptualization	Category
Ga4	The implementation of the education plan not only cultivates the students' autonomous learning ability, but also ensures the students' basic learning "formation", which lays a good foundation for the convergence of online and off-line learning. "Half of the students' learning effect is from teaching and half from learning. The focus of teaching is to teach students how to learn, and the cultivation of students' autonomous learning ability is the most important." Guo Qiang, a primary school mathematics researcher of Weifang High tech Zone Academy of Educational Sciences, said, "in the process of the implementation of the network public welfare classroom, the district promotes the use of the diploma design that can reflect the students' learning process and cultivate students' learning ability. On the one hand, it can evaluate the effect of online teaching, on the other hand, it also prepares for the organic connection of online and off-line teaching."	Z8: According to the actual learning effect of students in the early stage, the follow-up teaching should be arranged scientifically Z9: Guide the scientific formulation of the connection scheme of returning to school and returning to class teaching	

(Continued)

Table D1 (Continued) Examples of open coding and axial coding of policy

Coding Number	Original Statement	Conceptualization	Category
Ga5	"To do a good job in the organic connection between online teaching and off-line teaching after the beginning of school, unity and cooperation at all levels are crucial," Yang Shuping said. The District Academy of Educational Sciences, primary and secondary schools, and teaching and research teams of various disciplines should cooperate closely. The teaching and research staff should also guide teachers of various disciplines and make collective and individual supplementary plans according to the learning situation. Each teacher should formulate a feasible supplementary plan, so as to truly achieve the teaching objectives of the semester curriculum.	Z10: Overall adjustment of teaching arrangement Z11: Coordinate the teaching plan of all kinds of schools at all levels	
Ga6	The UNICEF representative office in China was willing to jointly launch the "safe return to school" with the Ministry of Education, and cooperate in developing posters and videos of epidemic prevention in primary and secondary schools, so as to fully cooperate with the relevant publicity and education after the start and resumption of classes.	Z12: According to the actual learning effect of students in the early stage, follow-up teaching should be arranged scientifically Z13: Guide the scientific formulation of the connection scheme for returning to school and returning to classroom teaching Z14: Overall adjustment of teaching arrangement Z15: Coordinate the teaching plans of all kinds of schools at all levels	

(*Continued*)

Coding Number	Original Statement	Conceptualization	Category
Ga7	The minister of the novel coronavirus pneumonia office is responsible for the work of the new leadership, and Chen Baosheng, Minister of the leading group of the Ministry of Education, thanked UNICEF for its support and evaluation of China's fight against the new crown pneumonia, and its concern and support for China's education, and its long-term concern and love for Chinese children. It was very meaningful for the two sides to jointly carry out the "safe return to school action". They would make use of the network platform of the education department to actively promote the posters and videos of epidemic prevention publicity in primary and secondary schools, distribute and post the posters to schools and kindergartens through local education departments, and strengthen epidemic prevention publicity and education for teachers and students. At present, the Ministry of Education is working out a health education program covering all kinds of schools at all levels. It is hoped that the United Nations Children's fund would provide active support in sports guidance, nutrition and health, food safety, school health, and other aspects.	Z16: Do a good job of psychological guidance for students Z17: Guide students to develop the consciousness of daily epidemic prevention Z18: Pay attention to students' eyesight and health Z19: A reasonable arrangement of students' work and rest schedule Z20: Strengthen teaching service management and attach importance to students' mental health counseling Z21: Do a good job of psychological guidance for students	

Table D1 (Continued) Examples of open coding and axial coding of policy

Coding Number	Original Statement	Conceptualization	Category
Ga8	Issued the notice on novel coronavirus pneumonia, the notice of the beginning of the spring semester in 2020, and the notice on further improving the prevention and control of the new crown pneumonia in schools, and put forward specific requirements for the preparatory work of all schools in various places. Carry out information sorting, comprehensively check the health codes of teachers, students, and staff before the start of school, distinguish the situation, and clarify the specific requirements. To guide all schools to develop work plans for faculty and students to return to school, require school administrators, head teachers, teachers, counselors and school doctors to arrive at their posts in advance one week before the start of school, reasonably set up the routes to enter the campus and arrangements for temperature detection, and make detailed plans for going to and from school at the wrong time to avoid students gathering. Led by the working committee of the provincial Party committee and the Provincial Department of Education, 14 on-the-spot supervision teams were formed to carry out supervision and inspection on the opening work of the city, prefecture, and relevant universities one week before the opening of school. It focuses on supervising and inspecting the preparation of teachers and students returning to school, the management of returning personnel, online education and teaching, the implementation of epidemic	Z22: Emergency plan for epidemic prevention on campus Z23: To coordinate the campus epidemic prevention and protection arrangements of all kinds of schools at all levels Z24: Strengthen the deployment of school opening work Z25: Strengthen the reserve of epidemic prevention materials	

Coding Number	Original Statement	Conceptualization	Category
	prevention and control measures, and continuously tracking and supervising the rectification of relevant problems, so as to ensure the smooth and orderly start of school. To guide all schools in strengthening research into the epidemic situation and estimation and material reserve calculation, and do a good job of epidemic prevention material reserve in advance and in an orderly manner. The Provincial Department of Education, together with the provincial Development and Reform Commission, the Department of Industry and Information Technology, the market supervision bureau (Drug Administration) and other relevant departments, set up special classes to strengthen the deployment of school masks. Increase funding support, allocate 35 million yuan to support the procurement of epidemic prevention and control materials for all levels and types of schools, and at the same time, clarify the prevention and control materials and funds required by colleges and universities and primary and secondary schools (kindergartens) in the province, and provide overall support according to the principle of hierarchical responsibility. The supply and demand docking channels should be unblocked, and a number of anti-epidemic materials production enterprises and purchase guarantee stores should be coordinated and contacted for autonomous purchase by various localities and universities. There are about 36 million masks, 300,000 temperature-measuring guns and 2,000 sets of thermal imaging equipment in the province and cities.		

(Continued)

Table D1 (Continued) Examples of open coding and axial coding of policy

Coding Number	Original Statement	Conceptualization	Category
Ga9	Guide all schools in formulating a practical education and teaching connection plan according to students' home learning situations during the extended opening period. For students who couldn't go to the university for the time being, and those who are still abroad, we should formulate special programs and do a good job in online learning guidance and psychological counseling. According to the development of online teaching, each city and state determines its own teaching plan for this semester to ensure that the required courses are fully opened and the teaching tasks of spring semester were completed with high-quality. Distinguish junior three, senior three, and other grades, reasonably arrange teaching time, pay attention to the combination of work and rest, in order to ensure rest time. We should conscientiously organize the "first lesson of returning to school", promote the anti-epidemic spirit in the classroom, and organize all students to have a patriotic education class, ideological and political theory class, patriotic health movement, and public health knowledge popularization class. In order to ensure the quality of teaching, it should guide local education departments and colleges to do a good job in teacher training and strengthen classroom management. According to the arrangement of the college entrance examination time extension, make a synchronous adjustment to the relevant examination time. Adjust the entrance examination of art majors in colleges and universities, print and	Z26: Strengthen the guidance of education and teaching Z27: Strengthen the overall planning of examination time Z28: Overall adjustment of teaching arrangements	

(*Continued*)

Coding Number	Original Statement	Conceptualization	Category
	distribute notices on doing a good job in the entrance examination of art majors under the epidemic situation, and guide colleges and universities in adjusting entrance examination methods scientifically. At present, the nine colleges and universities that originally planned to organize school examinations in other provinces have cancelled on-site school examinations, instead of enrolling students with the results of the unified examination in the province of origin, or organizing examinations off-site. At the same time, the time of individual enrollment examinations for higher vocational colleges was postponed. Adjust the examination time of junior high school and senior high school. The examination time of senior high school would be postponed to the end of the college entrance examination; In principle, the examination of junior high school academic level shall be arranged after the entrance examination. The time adjustment for the college entrance examination and the general high school academic level examination shall be conducted by all cities and states, and the local actual situation and the specific time arrangement shall be studied by themselves. The examination shall be timely announced to the society after being approved by the local Party committee and government and reported to the education department for record.		

Table D1 (Continued) Examples of open coding and axial coding of policy

Coding Number	Original Statement	Conceptualization	Category
Ga10	Printed and distributed the province's education system risk investigation program, specially deployed the risk investigation work before the beginning of school. To guide schools in strengthening their communication with health departments, disease control institutions, and hospitals, actively strive for professional and technical guidance, and strive to ensure the support of epidemic prevention personnel and material supply after the beginning of school. Under the guidance of the CDC department, colleges and universities are required to prepare emergency plans for campus public health events, which should be recorded and approved as the work plan for the start of school. To guide colleges and universities to strengthen the relevant skills training and emergency drills of teaching staff, so as to ensure the timely and effective disposal of emergencies and ensure the safety and stability of campus after the start of school.	Z29: Strengthen the preparation of emergency plan Z30: Emergency plan for campus epidemic prevention	

In order to identify the relationship between the initial concept and category, determine the main and secondary categories, use the combination of qualitative and quantitative methods to encode the principal axis, and calculate the percentage of each initial concept in the total number of samples, as shown in Table D2.

Table D2 The percentage of the initial concepts in the total sample numbers

Concept Number	Concept Name	Percentage (%)	Concept Number	Concept Name	Percentage (%)
Z1	Emergency plan for campus epidemic prevention	81.25	Z13	Pay attention to the problem of students' eyesight and health	48.39
Z2	Make overall arrangements for epidemic prevention and protection in all kinds of schools at all levels	78.13	Z14	It is necessary to arrange students' work and rest schedule reasonably	29.03
Z3	Release the notice of preparing to resume classes	62.5	Z15	Strengthen the management of teaching service and attach importance to the guidance of students' mental health	22.58
Z4	Adjust teaching arrangement in an overall way	16.12	Z16	Pay attention to the cultivation of students' awareness and ability of autonomous learning	41.94
Z5	Guide the scientific formulation of the connection scheme between the resumption of study and the resumption of teaching	59.38	Z17	Actively mobilize students' learning activity, initiative, and creativity	25.81
Z6	To make overall arrangements for the teaching plans of all kinds of schools at all levels	50	Z18	Monitor students' online learning	16.13
Z7	Continue to promote the relevant work of " Disrupted Class, Undisrupted Learning" before school starts	43.75	Z19	Provide guidance on the connection between the resumption of classes and online learning	15.63
Z8	Pay attention to the resumption of classes and schools for special groups	18.75	Z20	Hold lectures and forums on effective conversions between off-line teaching and online teaching provided by first-line teachers	29.03
Z9	Effectively carry out the transformation between online teaching and off-line teaching	62.5	Z21	Guide students to effectively carry out the conversion between off-line learning and online learning	41.94

Concept Number	Concept Name	Percentage (%)	Concept Number	Concept Name	Percentage (%)
Z10	According to the actual learning effect of students in the early stage, arrange the follow-up teaching scientifically	46.88	**Z22**	Through official accounts, etc., provide parents with relevant information on how to resume school	37.5
Z11	Make a good job of psychological instruction for students	37.5	**Z23**	Help students adjust their psychology	43.75
Z12	Help students develop the consciousness of daily epidemic prevention	15.63	**Z24**	Help students pay attention to daily epidemic prevention	18.75

Through the overall data analysis of Table D2, initial concepts that account for less than 20% are eliminated or integrated. Thus, the coding table of government entities with 24 countermeasures is obtained, as shown in Table D3.

Table D3 Coding table of the exiting period of the government

Subject	Level	Countermeasure	Proportion (%)
Schools	Organizations' Level	Emergency plan for campus epidemic prevention	81.25
		Make overall arrangements for epidemic prevention and protection in all schools	78.13
		Publish the notification of resumption of schools	62.5
		Make overall adjustment of teaching arrangement	16.12
		Conduct the scientific formulation for resuming teaching	59.38
		Arrange teaching plans for the resumption of all schools	50
		Continue to promote the relevant work of "Classes suspended but learning continues" before school starts	43.75
	Teachers' Level	Focus on special groups returning to schools	18.75
		Carry out the transformation between online teaching and off-line teaching effectively	62.5
		Arrange follow-up teaching scientifically, according to the actual learning effects of students in the early stages	46.88
		Do a good job of psychological instruction for students	37.5
		Help students to develop an awareness of daily epidemic prevention	15.63
	Students' Level	Pay attention to students' eyesight and health	48.39
		Arrange time of students properly	29.03
		Strengthen the management of teaching and attach importance to the guidance of students' psychological health	22.58
		Pay attention to the cultivation of students' awareness of and ability for autonomous learning	41.94
	Cultivate students' autonomous learning ability	Mobilize students' learning autonomy, initiative, and creativity	25.81
		Monitor students' online learning	16.13

(*Continued*)

Table D3 Coding table of the exiting period of the government

Subject	Level	Countermeasure	Proportion (%)
Enterprises	Organizations' Level	Provide instruction for the connection between the resumption of classes and online learning	
	Teachers' Level	Hold lectures and forums for frontline teachers to provide an effective conversion between off-line teaching and online teaching	
	Students' Level	Conduct students to effectively carry out the conversion between off-line learning and online learning	
	Families' Level	Provide parents with relevant information on how to cooperate with the schools through WeChat subscriptions	
Families		Help students adjust their psychology	43.75
		Help students pay attention to daily epidemic prevention	18.75

References

Atack, L., Parker, K., Rocchi, M., Maher, J., & Dryden, T. (2009). The impact of an online interprofessional course in disaster management competency and attitude towards interprofessional learning. *Journal of Interprofessional Care, 23*(6), 586–598. doi: 10.3109/13561820902886238.

Barnett, D. J., Everly, G. S., & Parker, C. L. (2005). Applying educational gaming to public health work force emergency preparedness. *American Journal of Preventive Medicine, 28*(04), 390–395. doi: 10.1016/j.amepre.2005.01.001

Baytiyeh, H. (2018). Online learning during post-earthquake school closures. *Disaster Prevention and Management, 27*(2), 215–227. doi: 10.1108/DPM-07-2017-0173

Baytiyeh, H. (2019). Why school resilience should be critical for the post-earthquake recovery of communities in divided societies. *Education and Urban Society, 55*(5), 693–711. doi: 10.1177/0013124517747035

Biocca, F., Harms, C., & Burgoon, J. K. (2003). Toward a more robust theory and measure of social presence: Review and suggested criteria. *Presence-Teleoperators and Virtual Environments, 12*(5), 456–480. doi: 10.1162/105474603322761270

Cadima, R., Ferreira, C., & Monguet, J. et al. (2010). Promoting social network awareness: A social network monitoring system. *Computers & Education, 54*(4), 1233–1240. doi: 10.1016/j.compedu.2009.11.009

Cao, J. (2014). *The development trend of catastrophe and its influence on the change of world insurance industry.* Master's thesis. Southwest Minzu University. Retrieved from https://kns8.cnki.net/kcms/detail/detail.aspx?FileName=1014069804.nh&DbName=CMFD2015

Cao, J., Fu, A., Wang, R., Zhou, L., & Huang, L. (2017). The effect of instructors' presentation types on students' social presence and learning outcome in the teaching video. *Modern Educational Technology, 27*(7), 75–81. Retrieved from https://kns.cnki.net/kcms/detail/detail.aspx?FileName=XJJS201707012&DbName=CJFQ2017

Chawla, D. S. (2018). Making children safer online. *Nature, 562*, S15. Retrieved from https://www.nature.com/articles/d41586-018-06848-6

Chen, B. (2020, April 21). Online education: Inequality between reality and ideal. *Chinese Journal of Science and Technology.* (6).

Chen, H., Lei, T., Zhan, C., Han, J., Yao, Z., & Wang, X. (2011). Research on emergency response mechanism and technical means of oil spill in the Gulf of Mexico and its enlightenment. *Ocean Development and Management, 28*(11), 51–54. Retrieved from https://kns.cnki.net/kcms/detail/detail.aspx?FileName=HKGL201111018&DbName=CJFQ2011

Chen, X., & Peng, H. (2020). Resilient China: Social welfare innovation and response to major crisis. Forum Summary. *Journal of Social Work*, (5), 104–107+112. Retrieved from https://kns.cnki.net/kcms/detail/detail.aspx?FileName=SHGO202 005013&DbName=CJFQ2020

China Education News Network. (2020) Suspension of school in some areas shows people-oriented. Retrieved from https://mp.weixin.qq.com/s/pzU9ytpC5Qqr5m MH24lHLg

Chinese iiMedia Research. (2020, March 27). Primary and secondary school online education industry operation monitoring report. Retrieved from https://www. iimedia.cn/c400/70402.html

Dahlstrom-Hakki, I., Alstad, Z., & Banerjee, M. (2020). Comparing synchronous and asynchronous online discussions for students with disabilities: The impact of social presence. *Computers & Education*, 150, 103842. doi: 10.1016/j.compedu.2020.103842

Dai, B., & Liu, Y. (2015). Examining users' intention to continue using WeChat based on the expectation-confirmation model, social presence and flow experience. *Journal of Modern Information*, *35*(03), 19–23. doi: 10.396h9/j.issn.1008-0821.2015.03.004

Ding, X. (2012). *Study on education emergency policy planning and mechanism construction—In the case of the Democratic Republic of the Congo.* Southwest University. Retrieved from https://kns.cnki.net/kcms/detail/detail.aspx?FileName= 1012342776.nh&DbName=CMFD2012

Enthoven, C. A., Tideman, J. W. L., Polling, J. R., Yang-Huang, J., Raat, H., & Klaver, C. C. (2020). The impact of computer use on myopia development in childhood: The Generation R study. *Preventive Medicine*, *132*, 105988. doi: 10.1016/j. ypmed.2020.105988

Evers, A. (1990). *Shifts in the welfare mix: Introducing a new approach for the study of transformations in welfare and social policy.* In A. Evers & H. Wintersberger (Eds.), *Shifts in the welfare mix: Their impact on work* (pp. 7–30). Social Services and Welfare Policies. Bloomington: Campus Verlag.

Fan, H., & Peng, H. (2019). An analysis of the needs for a better life and the innovation of social welfare system. *Journal of Anhui University (Philosophy and Social Sciences Edition)*, *43*(02), 126–134. Retrieved from https://kns.cnki.net/kcms/ detail/detail.aspx?FileName=ADZS201902015&DbName=CJFQ2019

Fu, W., & Zhou, H. (2020). Challenges brought by 2019-nCoV epidemic to online education in China and coping strategies. *Journal of Hebei Normal University (Educational Science)*. *22*(02), 14–18. Retrieved from https://kns8.cnki.net/kcms/ detail/detail.aspx?FileName=HSJY202002005&DbName=CJFQ2020.

Garrison, D. R., Anderson, T., & Archer, W. (1999). Critical inquiry in a text-based environment: Computer conferencing in higher education. *The Internet and Higher Education*, 2(2–3), 87–105. doi: 10.1016/S1096-7516(00)00016-6

Gu, Z. (2011). *The logic of institutional evolution: Based on cognitive evolution and intersubjectivity* (pp. 190–200). Beijing: Science Press. doi: 10.7666/d.y1032096

Gunawardena, C. N., & McIsaac, M. S. (2004). Distance education. In D. H. Jonassen (Ed.), *Handbook for research on educational communications and technology* (pp. 355–395). Mahwah, NJ: Lawrence Erlbaum Associates.

Han, Y. (2012). From welfare pluralism to welfare governance: Path evolution of welfare reform. *Social Sciences Abroad*, (2), 42–49. Retrieved from https://kns.cnki. net/kcms/detail/detail.aspx?FileName=GWSH201202008&DbName=CJFQ2012

Hansen, J. D., & Reich, J. (2015). Democratizing education? Examining access and usage patterns in massive open online courses. *Science*, *350*(6265), 1245–1248. doi: 10.1126/science.aab3782

Heidegger, Martin. (2011). *Lectures and essays*. Sun, Z., trans (p. 172). Beijing: Sanlian Bookstore.

Hou, J., & Li, M. (2013). Review and prospect of studies on natural disaster emergency management. *Journal of Institute of Disaster Prevention, 15*(01), 48–55. Retrieved from https://kns.cnki.net/kcms/detail/detail.aspx?FileName=FZJS201301010&Db Name=CJFQ2013

Hu, B. (2007). *Theoretical hypothesis and practice test of fact and value model of crisis communication management*. Beijing: China Renmin University Press (CRUP).

Huang, L. (2000). "Welfare State", "Welfare Pluralism" and "Welfare Marketization". *China Reform*, (10), 63–64. Retrieved from https://kns.cnki.net/kcms/detail/detail. aspx?FileName=ZGGG200010026&DbName=CJFQ2000

Huang, R. (2020a, March 7). Grasp the key elements to effectively promote online learning. *China Education Daily*, 3. Retrieved from http://www.jyb.cn/ rmtzgjyb/202003/t20200307_304283.html

Huang, R., Wang, Y., Wang, H., Lu, H., & Gao, B. (2020). The new instructional form of the future education: Flexible instruction and active learning. *Modern Distance Education Research, 32*(3), 3–14. Retrieved from https://kns.cnki.net/ kcms/detail/detail.aspx?FileName=XDYC202003001&DbName=CJFQ2020

Huang, W. (2020b, April 11). How does online education reduce the burden on parents: An interview with Professor Zhong Baichang of South China Normal University. *China Education Daily*, (3). Retrieved from http://www.jyb.cn/ rmtzgjyb/202004/t20200411_315941.html

Huang, W. (2020c, February 8). In the face of the epidemic, deep integration is the key to online learning: Interview with Professor Zhong Baichang and Zhan Zehui, doctoral supervisors of School of educational information technology, South China Normal University. *China Education Daily*, (3). Retrieved from http://www. jyb.cn/rmtzgjyb/202002/t20200208_292968.html

Johnson, N. (1999). *Mixed economies of welfare: A comparative perspective* (p. 5). London: Prentice Hall.

Kim, J. J. (2010). Developing an instrument to measure social presence in distance higher education. *British Journal of Educational Technology, 42*(5), 763–777. doi: 10.1111/j.1467-8535.2010.01107.x

Lanca, C., & Saw, S. M. (2020). The association between digital screen time and myopia: A systematic review. *Ophthalmic and Physiological Optics. 40*(2), 216–229. doi: 10.1111/opo.12657

Leh, A. S. C. (2001). Computer-mediated communication and social presence in a distance learning environment. *International Journal of Educational Telecommunications, 7*(2), 109–128. Retrieved March 21, 2021 from https://www.learntechlib.org/primary/ p/8470/.

Li, J. (2003). *Government crisis management*. Beijing: China City Press.

Li, J. (2012). Research on social support system of family education for migrant children from the perspective of welfare pluralism. *Journal of Socialist Theory Guide*, (11), 24–27. Retrieved from https://kns.cnki.net/kcms/detail/detail.aspx?File Name=LLDK201211009&DbName=CJFQ2012

Li, J. (2017). *Welfare diversity: A path to promote the development of inclusive society*. Master's thesis. Xinjiang University. Retrieved from https://kns.cnki.net/kcms/ detail/detail.aspx?FileName=1017712609.nh&DbName=CMFD2017

Li, W., & Zhu, Z. (2020). Improving affectional experience to alleviate emotional problems with online learning during a large-scale epidemic. *China Educational*

Technology, (5), 22–26,79. Retrieved from https://kns.cnki.net/kcms/detail/detail. aspx?FileName=ZDJY202005005&DbName=CJFQ2020

Liang, W. T., Chen, K. H., Wu, Y. F., Yen, E., & Chang, C. Y. (2016). Earthquake school in the cloud: Citizen seismologists in Taiwan. *Seismological Research Letters*, *87*(1), 177–185. doi: 10.1785/0220150061

Lin, M. (2002). The rise of welfare pluralism and its policy practice. *Chinese Journal of Sociology*, (7), 36–37. Retrieved from https://kns.cnki.net/kcms/detail/detail.asp x?FileName=SHEH200207013&DbName=CJFQ2002

Lin, M. (2015). China's social welfare development strategy: From negative to positive. *Journal of Chinese Academy of Governance*, (2), 73–78. Retrieved from https:// kns.cnki.net/kcms/detail/detail.aspx?FileName=LJXZ201502013&DbName=C JFQ2015

Lin, M. (2019). An outline of social security in the new era with a good life as the core. *Inner Mongolia Social Sciences*, *40*(3): 30–35+2. Retrieved from https://kns.cnki. net/kcms/detail/detail.aspx?FileName=NMGR201903005&DbName=CJFQ2019

Lin, M. (2020). On the positioning, relationship and realization of the multi-subject responsibility of social assistance. *Social Science Research*, (3), 97–101. Retrieved from https://kns.cnki.net/kcms/detail/detail.aspx?FileName=SHYJ202003010&D bName=CJFQ2020

Lin, M., & Liang, Y. (2019). A development history and overall trend to the social welfare system in china over the past 70 years. *Administration Reform*, (7), 4–12. Retrieved from https://kns.cnki.net/kcms/detail/detail.aspx?FileName=XZGL201 907001&DbName=CJFQ2019

Lin, M., & Wang, Z. (2001). Research on non-profit organizations from the perspective of welfare pluralism. *Social Science Research*, (6), 103–107. Retrieved from https:// kns.cnki.net/kcms/detail/detail.aspx?FileName=SHYJ200106025&DbName=C JFQ2001

Liu, M. (2020a). Accurate connection between online and offline: The key to improving education's ability to respond to disasters in the information age. *Journal of Curriculum and Instruction*, (3), 83–86. Retrieved from https://kns.cnki.net/kcms/ detail/detail.aspx?FileName=KEJY202003015&DbName=CJFN2020.

Liu, S. (2020b). Some thoughts about "Classes suspended but learning continue". *China Educational Technology*, (5), 7.

Liu, Y. (2020c). Thinking on ensuring substantial equivalence of quality between online teaching and off-line classroom teaching. *Education Teaching Forum*. (17), 325–326. Retrieved from https://kns8.cnki.net/kcms/detail/detail.aspx?FileName= JYJU202017153&DbName=CJFQ2020

Liu, Y., & Zhou, Q. (2012). Education in emergencies and reconstruction from the perspective of education for all: A review on minimum standards for education of INEE 2010. *Studies in Foreign Education*, *39*(06), 26–34. Retrieved from https://kns. cnki.net/kcms/detail/detail.aspx?FileName=WGJY201206005&DbName=C JFQ2012

Lomicka, L., & Lord, G. (2007). Social presence in virtual communities of foreign language (FL) teachers. *System*, *35*(2), 208–228. doi: 10.1016/j.system.2006.11.002

Ma, X. (2018). A comparison of Heidegger's and Aristotle's co existentialism. *Morality and Civilization*, (2): 51–58. Retrieved from http://www.ddywm.net/ddwm/ article/abstract/20180207?st=article_issue

Marco, M. D., Baker, M. L., et al. (2020). Opinion: Sustainable development must account for pandemic risk. *Proceedings of the National Academy of Sciences*, *117*(8), 3888–3892. doi: 10.1073/pnas.2001655117

Ministry of Education. (2020, January 29). How do children study at home after school is delayed? *The Ministry of Education: Use the online platform to "Disrupted Class, Undisrupted Learning"*. Retrieved from http://www.moe.gov.cn/jyb_xwfb/gzdt_gzdt/s5987/202001/t20200129_416993.html

Ministry of Education. (2020a, February 05). The Ministry of Education: More than 24,000 free open online courses are offered without suspension. *People's Daily Online*. Retrieved from http://edu.people.com.cn/n1/2020/0205/c1053-31572268.html.

Ministry of Education. (2020b, May 14). Ministry of Education: 17.75 million college students participated in online learning during the epidemic. *People's Daily Online*. Retrieved from http://edu.people.com.cn/n1/2020/0514/c1006-31709199.html

Ministry of Education. (n.d.) Using the online platform, "Disrupted Class, Undisrupted Learning". Retrieved from http://www.moe.gov.cn/jyb_xwfb/gzdt_gzdt/s5987/202001/t20200129_416993.html

Mirtoff, I., & Pearson, C. M. (1993). *Crisis management: Diagnostic guide for improving your organization's crisis-preparedness* (pp. 10–11). New York: Jossey-Bass Inc.

National Health Commission of China (NHC). (2019). Over half of the Chinese children and adolescents are short-sighted. *China News*. Retrieved from http://www.chinanews.com/jk/2019/04-29/8824266.shtml.

Norman, R. (2001). *Augustine crisis management*. Beijing: People's Publishing House.

O'Brien, G., O'Keefe, P., Rose, J., & Wisner, B. (2006). Climate change and disaster management. *Disasters*, *30*(1), 64–80. doi: 10.1111/j.1467-9523.2006.00307.x

OCHA. (2016, June 22). *Education Disrupted: Disaster Impacts on Education in the Asia Pacific region in 2015*. Retrieved from https://reliefweb.int/report/world/education-disrupted-disaster-impacts-education-asia-pacific-region-2015.

Paeka, H. J., & Hilyard, K. (2010). Theory-based approach and understanding public emergency preparedness: Implications for effective health and risk communication. *Journal of Health Communication: International Perspectives*, *15*(4), 428–444. doi: 10.1080/10810731003753083

Peng, H. (2006). Welfare Triangle: A paradigm of social policy analysis. *Sociological Studies*, (4), 157–168+245. Retrieved from https://kns.cnki.net/kcms/detail/detail.aspx?FileName=SHXJ200604008&DbName=CJFQ2006

Peng, H. (2020). The logic of globalization in social welfare: Criticism and reconstruction. *Journal of Social Development*, *7*(4), 17–29. Retrieved from https://kns.cnki.net/kcms/detail/detail.aspx?FileName=HFYJ202004002&DbName=CJFQ2020

Peng, H., & Huang, Y. (2006). Welfare pluralism: Welfare provision transformation from state to multi-sectors. *Nankai Journal (Philosophy, Literature and Social Science Edition)*, (6), 40–48. Retrieved from https://kns.cnki.net/kcms/detail/detail.aspx?FileName=LKXB200606005&DbName=CJFQ2006

People's Daily Online. (2020, March 19). *Grasping the industrial inflection point: New opportunities for industry development under the prevention and control of the epidemic – Seeking the development opportunities for online education in the post-epidemic era*. Retrieved from http://yuqing.people.com.cn/n1/2020/0319/c209043-31638772.html

People's Daily Online. (2021, August 28). *Under the premise of normalized epidemic prevention and control, nearly 300 million teachers and students will return to schools at the same time, according to the Ministry of Education – Ensure safe, normal and comprehensive opening of school*. Retrieved from http://edu.people.com.cn/n1/2020/0828/c1006-31839729.html

Ritchie, H., & Roser, M. (2020). "Natural Disasters". *Our WorldIn Data. org*. Retrieved from: https://ourworldindata.org/natural-disasters'

Robert, H., Wang, C., Song, B., & Jin, Y. (2004). *Crisis management*. Beijing: CITIC Publishing House.

Rogers, P., & Lea, M. (2005). Social presence in distributed group environments: The role of social identity. *Behaviour & Information Technology*, *24*(2), 151–158. doi: 10.1080/01449290410001723472

Rose, R. (1986). Common goals but different roles: The state's contribution to the welfare mix. In R. Rose & R. Shiratori (Eds.), *The welfare state East and West* (pp. 13–39). Oxford: Oxford University Press.

Ryuzawa, M. (1999). *Enterprise crisis management*. Shunde: GaoBao International Limited.

Sang, X. (2020). Warning of education in the COVID-19: Focus on habit and ability training. *Digital teaching in primary and secondary schools*. (5), 1. Retrieved from https://mp.weixin.qq.com/s/AzB3uwkeuJAIq-UxcgzEOA

Service, R. F. (2020a). Coronavirus epidemic snarls science worldwide. *Science (New York, NY)*, *367*(6480), 836–837. doi: 10.1126/science.367.6480.836

Service, R. F. (2020b). The disruption is enormous: "Coronavirus epidemic snarls science worldwide". *Science*, *367*(6480), 836–837. doi: 10.1126/science.367.6480.836

Shen, B., & Lin, M. (2020). The dynamics and trends of the research on social welfare attitudes. *Journal of Jiangxi University of Finance and Economics*, (6), 57–65. doi: 10.13676/j.cnki.cn36-1224/f.2020.06.007

Sheng, C., Liu, M., & Liu, G. (2019). The online group awareness-supported peer assessment system and its application. *Modern Distance Education Research*, *31*(4), 104–112. Retrieved from http://xdyjyj.scrtvu.net/zaiyao.asp?aid=4496&articleid=4496

Shi, Q. (2016). Discussion on the education of rural left-behind children from the perspective of welfare pluralism. *Business*, (4), 295. Retrieved from https://kns.cnki.net/kcms/detail/detail.aspx?FileName=SHNG201604237&DbName=CJFQ2016

Short, J., Williams, E., & Christie, B. (1976). *The social psychology of telecommunications*. London: John Wiley & Sons.

Strauss, A. (1987). *Qualitative analysis for social scientists*. Cambridge: Cambridge University Press. doi: 10.1017/CBO9780511557842

Tian, B., & Zhong, Z. (2009). The value idea of social welfare socialization: A four-dimensional analysis frame of welfare pluralism. *Exploration and Free Views*, (8), 44–47. Retrieved from https://kns.cnki.net/kcms/detail/detail.aspx?FileName=TSZM200908018&DbName=CJFQ2009

Tong, C., & Zhang, Y. (2018). The a research overview of the theory of welfare pluralism. *Social Welfare*, (5), 8–13. Retrieved from https://kns.cnki.net/kcms/detail/detail.aspx?FileName=MIZN201805003&DbName=CJFQ2018

Tonk, D., Weston, S., Wiley, D., & Barbour, M. K. (2013). Opening a new kind of high school: The story of the open high school of Utah. *International Review of Research in Open and Distance Learning*, *14*(1), 255–271. Retrieved from https://schlr.cnki.net/Detail/index/SJDJLAST/SJDJBF30269529B24B9CB5D182C337B5B146

Tu, C. H., & McIsaac, M. (2002). An examination of social presence to increase interaction in online classes. *American Journal of Distance Education*, *16*(3),131–150. Retrieved from https://www.learntechlib.org/p/119966/

UNESCO. (2020). COVID-19 educational disruption and response. Retrieved from https://en.unesco.org/themes/education-emergencies/coronavirus-school-closures.

UNESCO Bangkok. (2020a, June 16). COVID-19 and UNESCO: Monitoring the impact on people and places for relevant higher education. Retrieved from https://

bangkok.unesco.org/content/covid-19-and-unesco-monitoring-impact-people-and-places-relevant-higher-education

UNESCO Bangkok. (2020b, June 8). Reopen schools to secure learning and potential of an entire generation. Retrieved from https://bangkok.unesco.org/content/reopen-schools-secure-learning-and-potential-entire-generation

US Senate. (2006). *Committee on homeland security and governmental affairs.* Hurricane Katrina: A Nation Still Unprepared. Washington, DC: Government Printing Office.

Vagle, M. D. (2016). *Crafting phenomenological research* (p. 20). London: Routledge.

Wang, J., Wei, Y., & Zong, M. (2020). The current situation, problems and reflection of online teaching for primary and secondary school teachers during a large-scale epidemic: Based on the investigation and analysis of "classes suspended but learning continue" in Hubei Province. *China Educational Technology*, (5), 15–21. Retrieved from https://kns8.cnki.net/kcms/detail/detail.aspx?FileName=ZDJY202005004&DbName=CJFQ2020

Wang, P. (2020, April 24). Reform and innovation to improve the quality and efficiency of online teaching. *China Education Daily*, (2). Retrieved from http://www.jyb.cn/rmtzgjyb/202004/t20200424_320015.html

Wang, R. (2014). *Study of phased strategies of education in emergencies of Pakistan after earthquake.* Master's thesis. Southwest University. Retrieved from https://kns8.cnki.net/kcms/detail/detail.aspx?FileName=1014261371.nh&DbName=CMFD2014

Wang, X., & Zou, Y. (2008). Ecological aesthetics towards the ideal of symbiosis. *Seeker*, (9), 122–124. Retrieved from https://kns.cnki.net/kcms/detail/detail.aspx?FileName=QSZZ200809045&DbName=CJFQ2008

Wang, Y. (2010). Three analytical frameworks on Western social welfare. *Population and Development*, 16(06), 97–103. Retrieved from https://kns.cnki.net/kcms/detail/detail.aspx?FileName=SCRK201006018&DbName=CJFQ2010

Waugh, W. L. (2006). The political costs of failure in the Katrina and Rita disasters. *The Annals of the American Academy of Political and Social Science*, 604(1), 10–25. doi: 10.1177/0002716205284916

Webster, J., & Hackley, P. (1997). Teaching effectiveness in technology-mediated distance learning. *Academy of Management Journal*, 40(6), 1282–1309. doi: 10.5465/257034

Wei, J. (1994). Crisis and crisis management. *Management World*, (6), 53–59. Retrieved from https://kns.cnki.net/kcms/detail/detail.aspx?FileName=GLSJ199406012&DbName=CJFQ1994

Wisner, B., & Walker, P. (2005). Beyond Kobe: An interpretative report on the world conference on disaster reduction, Kobe, Japan, 18–22 January 2005. Retrieved from http://online.northumbria.ac.uk/geography_research/radix/resources/beyond_kobe_for_websites_july2005.pdf

WMO. (2013). Reducing and managing risks of disasters in a changing climate. *WMO Bulletin*, 62(Special Issue), 23–31.

Wu, D. (2020, February 22). Three difficulties and three misunderstandings of online teaching. *China Education Daily*, (3). Retrieved from http://www.jyb.cn/rmtzgjyb/202002/t20200222_298598.html

Wu, J., Fu, Y., Zhang, J., & Li, N. (2014). Meteorological disaster trend analysis in China: 1949–2013. *Journal of Natural Resources*, 29(09), 1520–1530. Retrieved from https://kns8.cnki.net/kcms/detail/detail.aspx?FileName=ZRZX201409007&DbName=CJFQ2014

Wu, L. (2010). *Preliminary research on the theory and practice of international emergence education*. Master's thesis. Henan University. Retrieved from https://kns.cnki. net/kcms/detail/detail.aspx?FileName=2010154925.nh&DbName=CMFD2010

Xie, L., & Zheng, B. (2003). *Basic theory of modern teaching* (pp. 204–205). Shanghai: Shanghai Education Press.

Xu, C., Wang, T., & Wang, Y. (2020). How to assure the quality of online education?: Methods and implications from APEC quality assurance of online learning toolkit. *Journal of World Education*. (4), 63–65. Retrieved from https://kns8.cnki.net/kcms/ detail/detail.aspx?FileName=JYXI202004016&DbName=CJFQ2020

Yang, G. Y., Huang, L. H., Schmid, K. L., Li, C. G., Chen, J. Y., He, G. H., & Chen, W. Q. (2020). Associations between screen exposure in early life and myopia amongst chinese preschoolers. *International Journal of Environmental Research and Public Health*, *17*, 1056. doi: 10.3390/ijerph17031056

Yang, X. (2020). The development trend and influence of online education under epidemic situation. *Dalian Daily*. (6). Retrieved from https://kns.cnki.net/kcms/ detail/detail.aspx?FileName=DLRB202004270062&DbName=CCND2020

Yin, H. (2009). *Research on the government emergency management of natural disasters in China*. Wuhan: Department of Administration, Central China Normal University.

Yu, J., & Gui, T. (2020, April 29). The British economy is looking for opportunities in the midst of an epidemic crisis. *International Business Daily*. (4). Retrieved from https://kns8.cnki.net/kcms/detail/detail.aspx?FileName=GJSB202004290042&Db Name=CCND2020

Yu, S., & Wang, H. (2020). How to better organize online learning in extreme environment such as epidemic situation. *Chinese Audio-Visual Education*, (5), 6–14+33. Retrieved from https://kns.cnki.net/kcms/detail/detail.aspx?FileName=ZD JY202005003&DbName=CJFQ2020

Zhan, Z., Mei, H.(2013). Academic self-concept and social presence in face-to-face and online learning: perceptions and effects on students' learning achievement and satisfaction across environments. Computers & Education, 69, 131-138. (SSCI, SCI index, Q1, Impact Factor= 2.881) https://doi.org/10.1016/j.compedu.2013.07.002

Zhan, Z., Fong, P. S.W., Mei, H., Chang, X., Liang, T., & Ma, Z. (2015). Sustainability education in massive open online courses: A content analysis approach. *Sustainability*, *7*(3), 2274–2300. doi: 10.3390/su7032274

Zhan, Z., Wei, Q., & Hong, J. C. (2021). Cellphone addiction during the Covid-19 outbreak: How online social anxiety and cyber danger belief mediate the influence of personality. Computers in Human Behavior, 121, 106790.

Zhang, H. (2020a). The development and existing problems of online education. *Computer Products and Circulation*, (5), 265. Retrieved from https://kns.cnki.net/ kcms/detail/detail.aspx?FileName=WXXJ202005253&DbName=CJFQ2020

Zhang, J., & Zhang, L. (2018). The virtue dimension of teaching excellence: Based on the perspective of "co-existence" relationship. *Journal of the Chinese Society of Education*, (3), 60–65. Retrieved from http://www.jcse.com.cn/CN/Y2018/V0/I3/60

Zhang, W. (2014). Research on higher education welfare system under the framework of welfare triangle. *Southeast Academic Research*, (3), 138–143. Retrieved from https://kns.cnki.net/kcms/detail/detail.aspx?FileName=DLXS201403020&DbNa me=CJFQ2014

Zhang, Z. (2020b, March 10). What shortcomings should education make up for when studying at home. *China Education Daily*, (4). Retrieved from http://www.jyb. cn/rmtzgjyb/202003/t20200310_305055.html

Zhang, Z. et al. (2020, April 29). Challenges and countermeasures for the resumption of anti-epidemic normalization in primary and secondary schools. *China Education Daily*, (4). Retrieved from http://www.jyb.cn/rmtzgjyb/202004/t20200429_321734. html

Zhao, S. (2020, April 21). Online education in european universities (Part 1). *Chinese Journal of Science and Technology*. (7). Retrieved from https://kns8.cnki.net/kcms/detail/detail.aspx?FileName=KXSB202004210071&DbName=CCND2020

Zhao, X. (2010). Research on education emergency response mechanism after sudden natural calamity: Take Wenchuan earthquake for example. *Journal of Chongqing University (Social Science Edition)*, *16*(6), 151–158. Retrieved from https://kns.cnki.net/kcms/detail/detail.aspx?FileName=CDSK201006029&DbName=CJFQ2010

Zhao, Y. (2014). Under smart city-based perspective emergency management of guangzhou public safety. Master's thesis. *South China University of Technology*, Retrieved from https://kns.cnki.net/kcms/detail/detail.aspx?FileName=1014065150.nh&DbName=CMFD2015

Zheng, Y. (2020). *Classroom can be so vivid* (p. 1). Beijing: China Renmin University Press.

Zhong, B., & Zhan, Z. (2020a, February 8). Deep integration is the key for online learning during the epidemic. *China Education News Network*. (3) Retrieved from http://www.jyb.cn/rmtzgjyb/202002/t20200208_292968.html.

Zhong, B., & Zhan, Z. (2020b). To be or not to be: The effect of online education on myopia. *Science*. Retrieved from https://science.sciencemag.org/content/367/6480/836/tab-e-letters.

Zhou, H. (2020a, June 1). Online and offline education should complement each other. *People's Livelihood Weekly*. Retrieved from http://www.msweekly.com/show.html?id=119947

Zhou, J. (2020b). Suspension, non-suspension, growth, non-postponement: On how to improve the efficiency of students' online learning at home. *Information Technology Education in Primary And Secondary Schools*.(4). Retrieved from https://kns.cnki.net/kcms/detail/detail.aspx?FileName=ZXJA202004015&DbName e=CJFN2020.

Zhou, Y., & Tang, X. (2012). A reflection on the welfare pluralism in Chinese context. *Academic Research*, (11), 56–62+159. Retrieved from https://kns.cnki.net/kcms/detail/detail.aspx?FileName=XSYJ201211011&DbName=CJFQ2012

Zhu, B. (1992). Communication, intersubjectivity and objectivity. *Philosophical Research*, (2), 19–28. Retrieved from https://kns.cnki.net/kcms/detail/detail.aspx?FileName=ZXYJ199202002&DbName=CJFQ1992

Zhu, Z., Guo, S., Wu, D., & Liu, S. (2020, March 17). The interpretation, key issues and countermeasures of the policy of "disrupted class, undisrupted learning". *China Educational Technology*. (4), 1–7. Retrieved from https://kns8.cnki.net/kcms/detail/detail.aspx?FileName=ZDJY202004024&DbName=CJFQ2020

Zhu, Z., & Peng, H. (2020). Omnimedia learning ecology: A practical solution to cope with schooling difficulties during a large-scale epidemic. *China Educational Technology*, (3), 1–6. Retrieved from https://kns8.cnki.net/kcms/detail/detail.aspx?FileName=ZDJY202003001&DbName=CJFQ2020.

Index

Page numbers in **Bold** refer to table; page numbers *Italics* refer to figure

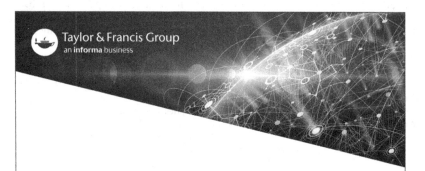

Printed in the United States
by Baker & Taylor Publisher Services